The Hypocrisy of Disco

The Hypocrisy of Disco

a memoir

by Clane Hayward

To Lisa- and to a part
of our lives when we ~~could talk~~ took
time to See + write + think + do.

Grateful to have that time
with a person like you, and
to see you now, good + happy

10/26/2019   ♡ ckn

For Ki, Haud, and Random.

None of this would have happened without Claude and Helene. None of it would have been written without Desmond Shea, Alison Alstrom, and Mike Taylor. It would not have been realized without Donald Pitschel and Peter Coyote. Thank you.

Chapter 1

Hogging the Covers

Slap bang goes the screen door three or four times, fast, because the seven of us kids are all leaving the house at once. Me and Andrew have an elbow fight, going Ow you dick and Shut up, turd. Haud and Matt jump off the porch saying Shazam, both their butt cracks showing whitely against the dusk of the night since they never, either one of them, pull up their pants right. Melena picks her way down the three steps carefully like a doe about to lose her balance. Scott and Cindy, who always wants to be called Cynthia, follow last.

We're going out to the school bus parked in the driveway to have a slumber party. It's early in the night and the air smells so good because it's just starting to rain. Northern California, where we live right now, smells this one way when it rains, the deepest green piney cool from the forest mixed with the muddy smell coming from the river which talks to itself a little way off. I can smell pennyroyal too, and I take big gulps of the air. The azaleas under the trees bloom pale blurs.

Together we make a sound of slapping tennies on dirt, of jeans and corduroys whistling, of gravel skipping ahead of our hurrying feet. We're all hushed and excited, whispering for no reason, fumbling at the door of the school bus, which gives a squeaky groan when Andrew opens it. I'm carrying extra blankets, Melena has candles and matches. Matt and Haud are shoving to get ahead of each other, and Scott runs down the aisle of the bus to flop on the big bed in the back. Cynthia has the flashlight and she keeps it on while we light candles and pile the blankets on the big bed and on the smaller bunk beds. I throw one of the blankets over Scott. I hit or kick or pinch him any time I can. Last week at his house we played spin the bottle. I really really really want to kiss him again.

The school bus is Matt and Melena and Andrew's mom's school bus and it's parked at my house for now. It has tables that unfold where there used to be seats, and cupboards and the bunk beds and a propane stove. Curtains go the length of the bus, strung on wires top and bottom, and there's a carpet in the aisle. The bus rocks a little when we run down the center of it and Andrew says, Don't, the candles will fall over. Matt makes an extra jump to show that Andrew can't boss him and then he tackles Haud and they wrestle clumsily. Haud and Matt, they're the squirmy puppy ones, always ratty and sleeping where they fall. Melena is scowly and picked on, and she always looks like she's just been pinched. Andrew's the bossy one with a big nose. Scott and Cynthia are always squabbling. I don't know for sure what I am because I'm in me and can't see me.

In age it goes Andrew, who's thirteen, and then Matt and Melena, who are twins, they're fraternal twins and they're ten. Not identical twins, Matt will sometimes say adamantly, and I'll say, No doy, otherwise you would look exactly alike. Scott and Cynthia are twelve and eleven, respectively. I'm Clane and Haud is my brother. I'm eleven and he's nine.

I've got Spanish fly, Scott says. We're all smushed together on the big bed and he's sitting on the edge and banging his feet on the cupboard underneath. What's Spanish fly? Melena and Cynthia ask, looking at each other and at me. Andrew looks up from the book he's trying to read in a pool of candlelight and says, It'll make you horny. It makes you want to hump. Melena scowls and Cynthia says, That just looks like rolled-up bread to me. I know it's just bread but I tell her no, really, it's Spanish fly, and she eats some even though she pretends she doesn't want to and starts rolling around on the bed. She bonks into me and I bonk into Andrew and he says quit it and then he grabs my hand and he hits me with my hand and goes, Why are you hitting yourself, huh? Why are hitting yourself? He always hits me and I know why, and I use this like my secret weapon against him. It's because if he likes me, and I know this, and he doesn't know I know this, then that makes me smarter than him.

Andrew and Matt and Melena and their little brother, Jude, and their mom, Susan, they live in a house near us, near me and Haud and our mom and our little sister, Ki. We live near the river in a vacation cabin even though we're not on vacation. Because it's cheaper, our mom says, even if it is a little chilly and dark. Scott and Cynthia live with their mom across town. We haven't lived here that long, we never live anywhere long, we move all of the time. We come and go with no explaining, and all the people I know come and go with no explaining either. Maybe the only thing I can explain in my life for sure is my name. When people ask how we got our funny names, and they always do, I say, with extra patience, Our dad is Claude and our mother is Helene and it goes Haud and Claude and Clane and Helene, get it? Then I say I also have a sister named Ki and a brother named Random, and they'll ask, *key* like in lock and key? and I say no. *Ki* means life force, it's Japanese. Random like, by chance? No, duh, Random like Random House.

Today was Passover and earlier we had a seder, all us kids and our moms and Susan's sister Serena and her little kid Shiva. There were bitter herbs and there was supposed to be a lamb bone but we didn't use one because we are all of us super-vegetarians, even though I wish we weren't. There was an argument about using the egg, too, and we used it but didn't eat it. The little kids got grape juice and we got grape juice mixed with wine. I'd never been to a seder before. I know that we're Jewish but I don't know what that's supposed to mean if we don't have passovers and Hanukkah or go to temple or say prayers at sundown. So Jewish is this religion but we're not religious like that. God is all one, Helene says, and so does the label on Dr. Bronner's peppermint soap. God is nowhere, God is now here, Helene says. Jesus was righteous and so was Mohammed and so was Buddha, and Bob Marley is a prophet. Helene is always saying, The forest is God, listen to the forest and listen to the mountain.

She will say this with her eyes closed and her hands clasped together, palms flat, after taking a big bong hit. She will breathe the smoke out in a big cloud and raise her arms up slow over her head and then she'll bring her palms together in front of her again.

She did this in the kitchen tonight when we had the seder, my mom all baked out on pot while we all scurried around holding bowls and plates and looking for spoons and chopsticks. Susan said, Who wants rice and who wants groats? and I picked groats and dove for the pot before Matt could. There was miso soup and tofu and vegetables too. Jude sat on the floor crying in his weird voice because he is deaf and dumb, holding a plate and tilting rice off it onto the floor, and Melena helped him stand up with his plate steadied. He's deaf and dumb but he's not retarded. We all ate at the table in the living room, which is low to the floor and has cushions around it instead of chairs. The smaller kids kneeled, wobbly, clutching spoons in their fists and picking dropped bits off the table. Ki sat on a cushion holding a bowl in her lap, eating very seriously with all her attention divided between one chubby grubby hand keeping the bowl from tipping over and the other hand getting a spoon too big for her into her mouth.

I liked the ceremony of seder, all of us there together. Susan made the blessings, one in Hebrew and one to Buddha and one to the goddess. Helene doesn't celebrate any holidays usually. She says Christmas is bourgeois and Thanksgiving is just dead turkey day. She says, Thanksgiving is a day when a large portion of the human planet will gather to celebrate the slaughtering, killing, cooking, and eating of the earth's creatures. Is that any way to honor the goddess, she asks? It is a strange reality some of us create and live in, she says merrily, eyes all glazed and dopey.

Ki tucked herself into my lap after she ate and busied herself with my shoelaces. She's two and a half and I love her so much. Her head beneath my chin smelled like dirty kid and sun and weeds and the incense that Helene and Susan always burn. Make some tea, Melena, Serena said, and Melena did it, scowling and bringing the teapot carefully to the table. Matt and Haud quibbled over the last carob brownie while Andrew read under a lamp and Susan and Helene started talking about their dumb guru. This is when we kids left for the school bus to have our slumber party. When they go on about Yakimoto Takagushi Scrotomushi Poopilashi and Steven Gaskin and the I Ching and the Grateful Dead they'll just go on forever.

In the school bus the candles throw dancey shadows in the corners. Haud takes the flashlight and makes his hands into a cup over the top and his hands glow pink. Andrew has the other flashlight and he puts it under his chin to make the light shine up eerily over his face and says, I am the true mastermind mwa ha ha ha. There's a little wind moving the tree branches outside and Scott goes, Did you hear that? I'm going to tell a ghost story, he says. There's this couple in a car that's stopped on the side of the road because they're out of gas. The man says, You wait here, I'm going to look for a gas station, and he leaves and disappears into the darkness. I've heard this one about a million times, Andrew says, sighing loud. Go back to your book, egghead, Cynthia says. What's an egghead? I want to know. Scott goes on impatiently. The man doesn't come back and doesn't come back and doesn't come back. All night. The woman sits in the car and hears the tree branches scraping the roof of the car, and the rain goes drip drip drip. In the morning the woman gets out of the car and what she finds is the man hanging from a tree over the car and it was his feet scraping on the roof all night, and his throat is cut and that's what made the dripping sound all night. We heard that one at camp, Cynthia says. Camp was so great, she says, eyes closed in ecstasy. There were boats and crafts and ghost stories around the fire. Are there horses? Haud wants to know, and what did you get to eat? I want to know. Marshmallows, Cynthia hollers, jumping up on the bed and making the whole bus rock.

Matt and Haud wrangle over who gets the top bunk and Melena is already asleep curled up in a little ball, and then Matt is asleep too and snoring. Haud in the top bunk kicks at the ceiling. I have to figure out how to sleep near Scott but not near Andrew in the big bed, and I get Scott on one side and Cynthia on the other side of me and Andrew on the other side of Scott. We sing a Beatles song quietly, "Rocky Raccoon." Andrew says, Quit hogging the covers, and Scott kisses me quietly under the blankets and his mouth is warm and too wet and I like his breath on my face. This is my life in 1978 in Northern California.

Chapter 2

Nothing in My Life Moves in Straight Lines

It's some day of the week but I don't know which one for sure because there's no reason to keep track of them. Melena is at my house and we're coloring in a Mayan calendar coloring book that I wish was a Barbie and Ken coloring book but Helene won't let me have a Barbie and Ken one. It's summer now. I haven't seen much of Matt and Melena and Andrew and Jude because they got to go to a summer camp and me and Haud didn't, and they got to go to Mexico and we didn't. I spent the summer reading at the library. Sometimes Helene took us to the river, and sometimes she took us to the movies. I read D'Aulaire's *Greek Mythology* and all of the *Little House on the Prairie* books and the Madeline L'Engle books *A Wrinkle in Time* and *A Wind in the Door*.

Melena and I are talking, our heads bent over the book and our hair falling over our faces like curtains, sloppy and tangly. Melena wants to know where me and Haud moved from, where were we before we came here and met her and Matt and Andrew and Jude. Where we are now is called Monte Rio, a little town along the Russian River not far from San Francisco.

I have to think for a minute when she asks this because why we are here and how we got here is a thing which is never clear to me. We move all of the time and it's been like this my whole life. Helene says it's because she's a gypsy. I have pictures in my head of all the places I've ever lived and some of them don't make any sense to me. I don't know how to explain any of this to Melena because then she will think we are weird. Which is true. We are weird. But so far it seems like Melena's family is almost, not quite but almost, as weird.

First we lived in San Francisco, I tell Melena, reaching over her to get a pencil called magenta for my coloring. We lived in San Francisco, where I was born, and Claude and Helene were together then. I was born just before the Summer of Love, I tell her. What's the Summer of Love? I don't know, I say, shrugging, it's just always what my mom says. My mom and dad met doing acid in North Beach with the Beats. What's acid? she asks. What's Beats? Where's North Beach? I'm not positive, I say, but I was born in March and I'm a Pisces. I tell Melena what Pisces is.

Helene does astrology and she says Pisces is a heavy trip, she says I was born under heavy stars. She will sit cross-legged on the floor with a blanket spread over her knees and a needle in one hand, wearing little round glasses with gold rims that she uses to see things up close. With her glasses on the edge of her nose and her nose wrinkled to keep the glasses up, she embroiders the signs of the astrological calendar onto the blanket. She shows them to me, saying, This is Cancer the crab and it's a water sign. This is Leo the lion and it's a fire sign. Pisces are the fish chasing each other, and that's you, Clanie. I should have waited a few days to have you, man, you were born under some heavy trips. You're a Pisces which is a mutable negative water sign. This means you are unstable. You have your moon in Capricorn and this means contradiction. You have your intuition in the house of time and will and responsibility. You have your emotion in the house of karma. You have your Venus in Scorpio and this is intense, Scorpio is the image of sudden death and inexplicable violence. You have a lot of planets retrograde.

Helene is doing her embroidery while we color, and Ki chews on a pencil and then on a rice cake I give her. The embroidery is always beautiful at first, rivers of green and purple and blue and violet silk running into each other round the two fishes swimming opposite. But, and there's always a but about my mother, she also puts pot leaves and mandalas and what she calls cosmic cats in the design too and this makes it look all hippie. My mom's wild mane of hair falls over the blanket on her knees and over the brown-green carpet covered in cat fur and crumbs of old food. Her dirty gnarled feet poke out of her Indian print skirts. She looks like a matted, witchy, *witch*.

What was San Francisco like, do you remember it? Melena asks me. I don't remember being a baby, doy, but I remember Haud being a baby, bouncing in a swing that hung from the ceiling. We stayed in a storefront where we lived with some other hippies and people called Diggers, and they all had tangled beards and shouted all the time. The noisy rivers of tie-dye people in San Francisco in the Haight. Rooms in the city with high ceilings painted in laughing cherubs, and in the rooms men wearing women's clothes, and the sound of their voices speaking high and whispery. Was the Diggers a commune? Melena asks. Yeah, and I lived in other communes too, the Hog Farm one, the one in Covelo, the one where Haud was born in Forest Knolls.

So we lived in San Francisco, I continue to Melena. But then we moved because the cities were going to go up in flames. Claude and Helene said the cities were going to burn in the aftermath of the movement, the Black Panthers fighting with the Diggers, the men fighting the women, people in the streets throwing rocks. America is eating its young. So we moved to some communes in the country and this I remember, snow on the ground and eating from cans. It was near Covelo and it was just called The Land. Us kids ran around naked in the dirt in summer, and I learned my first curse words. We said fuck and I even knew what fucking was and saw people doing it. Scary and gross.

I remember my mother and father were still together and then they weren't, and my dad left to go to another commune in New Mexico with another lady. I remember this hazy and not in a straight line. Nothing in my life moves in straight lines. We would be in California and then we would be in New Mexico, and then my dad had a new old lady and my mom had a new old man. One of them would be there and then gone and then there and then gone again, and then the other one would do the same. Claude's new old lady was named Mal and that's how I have a brother in New Mexico named Random, and Helene's new old man was named Bruce and that's how I have Ki. Random lives with his mom and I'm not sure where our dad is, New Mexico, too I think. Ki lives here with us and we don't know where her dad is. Matt and Melena and Andrew and Jude, they don't know for sure where their dads are, although Matt and Melena's dad might be in Peru, Machu Picchu. Because Matt and Melena and Jude have one dad and Andrew has a different dad. How come there's so many of us kids with our parents spread all over the place having different kids everywhere they go? I ask Helene. Helene says, Free love, man. Be fruitful and multiply across this earth. I haven't seen my dad for a few years.

Helene says, Clanie, make us a pot of rice and go see if Haud is around. I sigh heavily and put down my pencil and roll my eyes at Melena, who rolls hers back. She follows me to the kitchen which like the rest of our house is small and dark and a little damp, being right on the river. I measure two cups of brown rice and four cups of water into the enamel rice pot that I have to wash first because it's been sitting in the sink with the other dishes. Melena doesn't say anything about the dishes or the crumbs or the cat fur or your mom's a slob, and I feel hopeful about making friends with her and that is a new one.

We run outside banging the screen door and yelling for Haud, who comes half-running half-stumbling down the hillside near the house, his clothes and hair covered in pine needles. I was eating poison oak, Haud says triumphantly. If you eat the littlest red leaves you build up immunity to poison oak and you won't itch. Won't the inside of your mouth get it? Melena asks skeptically. Haud shakes his head vigorously like a dog throwing water off its coat. I say, Let's go see if we can play Jeffrey and Patrick's records. The three of us walk around the corner of the house to the little cabin where Jeffrey and Patrick live and bang on the door. They're not home so we sneak in. Haud pulls a chair over to the counter in the kitchenette and stands on it to reach a bag of sugar in the cupboard and we take turns pouring white sugar into each others' mouths. Helene won't have any sugar in the house and she keeps the honey jar hidden in her room so we won't sneak it but we do anyway. We play records, jumping around wild being different Beatles, I get to be Paul. Hold you in his armchair you can feel his disease, the Beatles sing, come together.

Jeffrey and Patrick come into their house, not mad to see us, saying, Oh you pretty things. They are tall and skinny and have long hair and wear high boots and lace. Jeffrey says Patrick is his lover and he says it *lovair*. It's near dark, it gets dark early under the redwoods, and Melena has to go, looking small under the trees as she walks home, almost invisible in the dense forest.

Chapter 3

Chew Each Mouthful Twenty Times

On another day that I don't bother to keep track of Helene says suddenly, like she just remembered it, You kids are starting school tomorrow. This is big, this is huge, because we hardly ever go to school. Schools are just zoos run by the government to keep kids safe in cages, Helene always says. Nine in the morning, she says, you catch the bus at the fork in the road where that big stump is. Me and Haud look up at her from our books all excited. She looks at us sourly and says, You're going to read lies printed on dead trees. Straightsville. Knock yourself out, whoopee, rolling her eyes and waving her finger in a circle in the air. But I'm immune to her sarcasm because school means we get hot lunch and I'm a big big big fan of school hot lunch. Hot lunch and clothes that match. If this is what being straight means, I want to be straight. Right away I start planning my outfit for tomorrow and right away we start fighting.

In town in front of the Community Store across the street from Bartlett's near the Pink Elephant there's a free box and I had found a pair of green bell bottoms in it. Like with no tears or rips, new. I ask Helene can I wear them, and she says, What about your overalls instead? What about your overalls with the pansies I embroidered on the knees? I don't want to wear those, they look like boy clothes. Well, what about your purple tie-dye? It's too hippie. I'm NOT going to wear tai chi shoes or tie-dye. Helene rolls her eyes and I know not to stay on the subject. If I don't argue with her about clothes maybe we won't get around to arguing about hot lunch and I need to protect the possibility of hot lunch no matter what. Helene won't let us wear clothes made from rayon or polyester, only natural fibers, and no Day-Glo colors. She makes us jackets out of old blankets and those are the worst. Look, I embroidered a cat singing to the moon on it for you. I once left mine on a bus on purpose.

I've been to schools before in different places we lived, but never for really long. I went to first grade when I stayed with Claude in New Mexico. I wanted to dress nice for my first day then, too, and I picked my favorite clothes: the ballerina dress with the wide skirt that stood out with netting, my purple hat with the purple ribbon in it, my orange plaid coat with the big buckle in the back. Boots for the snow. I didn't last very long at that school. It was in Peñasco. I had some trouble with the bigger kids who stole my hat, and someone said they burnt it because I had lice. But I didn't, that was before when I had lice. I don't think I had them this time. But at this school in Peñasco, one day the principal called me into the office. Who dresses you? he asked carefully. I dress myself, I said proudly. I didn't go to that school anymore after Christmas break and after my hat was maybe burnt. Claude didn't care. I wore my ballerina skirt until it just fell apart.

I'm awake early in the morning for school and I carefully brush my hair again and again, which is long and dark and always tangly. Haud doesn't brush his and squirms away when I try to brush it for him. We both have big dark eyes, his dark like coffee and mine with green and yellow specks in them. I make lunches for us, tofu sandwiches on lumpy homemade bread, with miso spread on the bread. No way am I going to eat this lunch if I can help it, but Helene will notice if I don't take it to school. When we get on the bus Haud runs down the aisle and flops into a seat singing to himself, Bang bang Maxwell's silver hammer came down on his head. The bus rumbles off slowly and a kid sitting behind me says, Why do you have all that stuff on your pants, and he means the pansies that peek through a hole in the knee that Helene embroidered.

Fourth grade. So this is how it goes for a few weeks: I have my homeroom class where we draw, paint, and read from a textbook of social studies about Washington and Lincoln and Jefferson and John F. Kennedy. Then recess, where I wander around on the playground watching other kids play. Then we do science and then we find things on maps. Then lunch. Lunch is so so so great. Then the rest of the class does math and I go to a different room for math because I don't know how to do math yet really and I'm way behind. Then I go to another different room for reading because I read so well that I'm way ahead.

Okay, did I say about lunch? First I love the cafeteria because it's warm and smells good. Then I love lunch because of the package it comes in. There's the hot part and the cold part, plus a carton of milk, too, regular or chocolate. The cold part comes in a little plastic tray that has compartments in it for salad and dessert and a packet with a spork and a napkin. The hot part comes in a cardboard container covered in foil. Then I love lunch because of what we get to eat. There's corn dogs and spaghetti and hamburgers and pizza and burritos and tacos and lasagna. It doesn't matter what it is, I'll like it. I'll eat mine and then I'll say to the person next to me, If you don't want your hamburger, I'll take it. No matter what it is, I'll eat it, and I eat it fast because we're not allowed it, me and Haud.

We're not allowed anything that comes in cafeteria lunches, not the milk or bananas or hot dogs or potato chips. I have been hungry for as long as I can remember and it's not because we don't have food. It's because Helene is a hippie and not just a vegetarian hippie but a macrobiotic hippie. Helene's kind of vegetarian means no butter or cheese or milk or eggs because they're from animals, even though they're not meat. Macrobiotic means no oranges or tomatoes because they're too acidic and unbalance your system. No tuna fish or blueberries or peanut butter. This is one other thing I know for sure besides how I got my funny name, the things we can't have. The thing I think about most is what I wish we could have, and it starts with cookies and ends somewhere around shoes. There are lots of things in the world between cookies and shoes. Hair ribbons and little purses and ice cream. Beach balls and necklaces and Oreos. Strawberry jam and tennies, new ones, and a pink backpack with zipper pockets.

Helene wasn't always macrobiotic. She used to be just vegetarian. Vegetarian, the normal kind, I can handle. Soyburgers with mayonnaise, corn chips, bean and cheese burritos, oatmeal cookies. We had curry at the Good Karma Cafe in San Francisco once, and rice pudding. Helene turned macrobiotic around the time Ki was born. She switched to macrobiotic with Ki's dad, Bruce. This was when I was maybe eight. But I first knew Bruce when I was six.

I met Bruce when I was six and in New Mexico and me and Haud were living with Claude and Mal. Mal for Madeline. Madeline Lovejoy, who named Random and named him Random Comet Lovejoy. Helene had been gone for a long time, long enough for me to sort of forget her. But when she showed up at the door I knew who she was. She did that, just showed up. She was at the door of Mal's house with her long witchy hair and her bare feet and she had a look on her face like, Hey, remember me? I'm back now. A crooked smile that said how great it was that she would turn up just like that. Look what the universe dragged in.

She had Bruce with her and he stood a little behind her, a guy who looked younger than her, with long blond hair and another crooked smile. Right away I didn't like Bruce, but too bad. You and Haud are coming to live with me and your mom now, 'kay? Bruce said, with his crooked smile and his chin tucked into his neck a little which is a thing he always did. We left New Mexico and went back to California.

We lived in a lot of places, as usual. First Cotati, which is near Santa Rosa and Sebastopol. Ki wasn't born yet. We lived in Sonoma Grove Trailer Park, and this was where the macrobiotic thing started. It happened all of a sudden. One day we went into Cotati for soyburgers with mayonnaise and tomatoes all dripping juice and making the burger into a squishy delicious mess in my hand, and the next day it was like soyburgers never existed. Not just that I couldn't have one, but that they just never were and never would be ever again.

After this we got the weirdest, dullest, worstest food I'd ever tasted. Remember to chew each mouthful twenty times, Helene said one day, handing me a bowl of rice and disgusting black things that looked like worms and tasted like old fish. Seaweed. Haud and I looked at our bowls in mute horror and we wouldn't eat, and Bruce wouldn't let us get up from the table until we ate something, so we sat there for hours. Every little thing was a battle after this. Can I have some more tamari on my rice? I would ask, looking up at Bruce desperately, and he would say, No, tamari is yang and you're too yang already. But Haud got more than me, I would say, and Helene would say, Haud is yin so he can have more yang things.

This was a hard time, in the trailer park in Cotati, when we turned macrobiotic. I was used to being a little hungry sometimes because it was never a sure thing when it was time for breakfasts or dinners or something like that. Claude didn't really cook dinner and we would whine that there was nothing to eat and he'd say, Waddya mean there's nothing to eat? There's cheese, there's bread, there's peanut butter, make yourselves sandwiches. But this was new. Macrobiotic just took over our life. There wasn't a thing that it didn't cover. Like no sleeping on your stomach or your sides, because only sick people and animals sleep on their stomachs; healthy people sleep on their backs. No drinking extra water from the faucet when you're brushing your teeth because water creates cravings for salt and this is an unbalance to your system. Only two squares of toilet paper when you go to the bathroom because a healthy person with a balanced system doesn't need to wipe more.

So I spent most of my time then, when I was six, wandering around the trailer park looking for other food and hoping Bruce wouldn't catch me. When he caught me eating a peanut butter sandwich with raisins in it at the neighbors I used all of my punishment time wishing he was dead. There was a lot of punishment time, usually under the covers in bed without supper.

Fortunately Bruce and Helene split up. This was right after Ki was born. We were living in San Rafael at someone's house and I was playing with a slinky on the steps only the slinky was broken, and Bruce came down the stairs with his chin tucked into his neck and said, Remember that five dollars Grandma Lynn gave you for your birthday? Uh-huh, I said, wary of him and for some reason embarrassed for him. Let me borrow it, 'kay? I gave it to him and I haven't seen him since. That's fine.

Helene is still just as bad macrobiotic but Haud and I are older now and we know how to sneak better. You're not eating that cafeteria shitfood, are you? she asked me a few days ago, and I said no, but I check the couch for quarters every day to buy hot lunch. If there aren't any quarters in the couch, I steal them from her purse. If I can't steal them from her purse and can't buy lunch, school isn't so great. It makes me feel droopy and sorry for myself. The math classes I don't understand, the reading classes that are too easy and boring, and the kids not talking to me except to ask, Why don't you brush your hair? Or, Why are you wearing that?

I don't think Haud likes school either. Does not play well with others, it says on his report card, and it says this because he stole someone's play handcuffs and handcuffed himself to a desk and when the teacher said, If you can't control your behavior, Haud, I don't want you in my classroom. Haud said okay and clumped the desk outside, still handcuffed to it, and clumped himself up and down the hall. He's always doing things like that, things that are weird but really funny too. Some days he'll say, Today all day I'm a rabid dog. He'll drool out of the side of his mouth and quiver, with his eyes rolled back in his head. He doesn't know the rules.

The school bus drops us off at the start of a narrow tarmac road that winds through the redwood forest. It's very quiet, just the wind talking to the trees and the sound of our tennies on the carpet of fir and redwood sprigs that lines the road. At lunch I wanted this girl's brownie so bad that first I asked her if we could be friends, and when she said yes I said, Well now that we're friends, can I have your brownie? She looked at me like, You're sooooo low. I think about this, walking home, and I also think about how Sean tagged me and danced around me, jumping up in the air and yelling, Girl germs girl germs, waiting for me to chase him.

There's no traffic, not many people live here. All along the road are little vacation cottages like ours. There are trash cans outside the little houses, and once I saw a bag of cookies poking out of the trash and I took it and gave some to Haud and we ate cookies as fast as we could all the way home. Even though they were from the trash they weren't dirty. The cottages are mostly empty except in the summer, I think because no one would want to live all year around under this damp dark blanket of forest. No sun can find its way in through the trees, and the ferns and rhododendron seem dank and spidery. We're on our way home to the smell of miso soup and kerosene lamps and old furniture, and Ki, when she sees me, will put her arms up in the air to be held, and her hair will smell like sweet dirty kid.

Chapter 4
Monte Rio Vacation Wonderland

We live in Monte Rio, near Guerneville, in Northern California. We have lived in a whole bunch of little towns all in this same area, and it is this area, the way it looks and smells and feels, that means California to me. It is the dusty trees along the side of the road that I dream about when I am in another place and another life. It is the smell of pennyroyal growing near the creek, of warm weeds baking in the sun and giving off their own wild green-y honey smell. California means low rolling hills covered in purple vetch in spring and brown grass in late summer and clumps of oak trees that look wise and patient and lonely. California means driving along narrow roads that wind through little towns like this, with the windows open to catch the smells, and the air goes cold warm cold warm as you drive through the shady parts and then back out into the sun.

Monte Rio sits along one of these narrow winding roads, in the middle of a redwood forest. You're driving through Guerneville and Rio Nido on River Road with the air changing temperature and then it's bright hot all of a sudden and you're at Monte Rio's only real intersection, with a big sign arching over the road saying, Welcome to Monte Rio Vacation Wonderland. Monte Rio is an odd tilty little town, the hot bright main street turning back into dim cool redwood lanes lined with dainty cottages looking like dwarves' houses beneath the towering forest. The light at the intersection looks all hot and bleached, all flooded with the sun bouncing off the tin-can-lying-on-its-side movie theater. Tonight we're going there to see a movie, *Yellow Submarine*, all of us kids and the moms too.

The road to the right takes you to Jenner and then the coast, and the road to the left, just after the movie theater, takes you across the bridge over the Russian River and into town where there's Bartlett's department store and the Rainbow Co-op and the Pink Elephant. The Pink Elephant smells, not badly, of beer and dusty carpet and is painted a chalky pink. It sort of leans on stilts over the river below it. A lot of the houses in Monte Rio are built over the river or up into the hillside and it's the stilts that keep them propped up. A lot of them are old so like they lean.

Bartlett's sells tools and toys and clothes and "groceries, beer, and liquor," which means shitfood that I'd kill for any day— Lay's potato chips or Vienna sausages. In front of Bartlett's, men wearing overalls and baseball caps slam in and out of pickup trucks or drink Pepsis on the cement porch. The Rainbow Co-op sells tamari chips and yinnie sandwiches and bulk buckwheat groats. In front of the Co-op, men with long hair and bare feet and tie-dyed shirts work over the open rear hoods of Volkswagen buses, and women with long hair and bare feet and tie-dyed skirts sort through piles of clothes in the free box.

Me and Melena are sitting on the curb in front of the Rainbow Co-op today watching Jude and Ki while Susan and Helene shop. They got their food stamps today. We're squatting on the curb and I have Ki sitting in the circle of my arms and legs. When she squirms to get out I squish her and she squeaks like a little mouse, and I pet her hair but don't let her go. Melena has her arm around Jude and he sits quietly like he's in a daze, which he usually is, his slanty eyes half closed in the sunlight, sometimes making his small grunting noises. Matt and Haud are howling and dancing around in the free box. They found a smushed basketball and they're stomping on it. Andrew is reading a book in the front seat of Susan's van.

We're comparing schools. Melena and Andrew and Matt go to Monte Rio Alternative, which is called the Free School, which is just down the road. Why is it called the Free School? I want to know. My school is free too. Melena shrugs. It's free because, because, you're free there, she says. Like, we don't have teachers, or classes, or homework. What do you do all day? She shrugs again and her face looks extra pinched while she thinks. We do projects and have talking circles and play games. I can do macrame and crochet. I made a God's eye. I know how to do batik. You're so lucky, I say. I hate school now. I was eating hot lunch in the cafeteria when Helene caught me, I say, and Melena's eyebrows raise so high they go all the way up into her hairline and she looks extra worried for a minute. But you aren't supposed to eat hot lunch, she breathes, swiping her bangs out of her eyes. I wish I could have bangs, I think, and I tell her the story of how Helene came into the cafeteria and caught me eating hot lunch, and how getting caught wasn't as bad as her just coming there, coming to my school. Helene had sailed down the main aisle of the cafeteria with Ki trailing along, Ki wearing a scared look because of all the kids around and Helene with a goofy stoned smile, the beads and feathers in her hair flopping around her bare shoulders and droopy boobs. She was wearing two layers of skirts over tai chi pants and her scaly heels hung over the back of her smushed shoes. The shoes, Chinese slippers, flopped on her feet and slapped the green linoleum , echoing across the whole cafeteria. A wave of silence rolled across the room as the kids watched her come, sporks raised halfway to their mouths and eyes opened wide. I was just frozen with embarrassment. I came to see your school, Clanie, she said, and I brought you a thermos of miso soup. I was just mute, looking at the burrito on my tray like, How did that get there? The next thing, we were on the road walking home and she was tugging me along by the collar of my shirt, saying, Clane I don't know what your trip is. I want you to be Cleopatra but you want to be Minnie Mouse.

When I finish telling her the story Melena nods her head like she knows just what I'm talking about. Melena and Matthew and Andrew have the same problems me and Haud do. What do you eat for lunch? I ask her. Susan makes our lunches, Melena says. Matt sits down next to her on the curb in front of the Co-op, panting, his greasy bangs sticking to the sweat on his forehead, while Haud sits down on the mashed basketball and pretends he's a dog, panting with his tongue lolling out. Susan's in a bean stage, Matt says. All we get is bean sandwiches, he sighs, and Melena sighs too. Homemade bread cut all thick and uneven, with mashed beans inside. That's worse even than a tofu sandwich, I breathe in disbelief. Andrew sits down next to me and puts a strip of macrame with beads on it carefully into his book to hold his place. He says, Yeah, but tofu starts problems too. Like how when other kids ask what kind of sandwich is that and you say tofu, they say, Toe food? and then they crack up. Yeah, yeah, we all chime in, and then we're all solemn and quiet for a minute, thinking about our problems.

Melena has big brown eyes that slant a little in a thin dark face, eyes a darker brown than mine, less hazel and more chocolate. She has limp scraggly dark hair and thin arms with thick hairs. Matt has dark eyes colored maybe like coffee, a little paler at the edges, and the same color hair but going blond at the tips, and his hair always looks like he just got out of bed. He has a round mouth like a girl's and rounder eyes than Melena too. They are both of them wearing shirts from Mexico, white cotton shirts with flowers embroidered on them. Matt doesn't care that his clothes look like girl clothes. Andrew has black curly hair and a big nose always poked into a book. He never says much, only to boss us or correct us. Jude never says anything, only sometimes making moans and gibbers. He's six but is the size of a four-year-old, his arms and legs as thin as sticks. He looks like an elf from outer space, with pointy ears and slanted eyes in a flat face with a narrow chin. I'm not laughing at him, I never do. He moves carefully like he's testing the air around him with a sonar that only deaf people have.

Susan and Helene come out of the Co-op carrying bulging wrinkled bags of broccoli and rice cakes and millet, bags of soy milk powder and bunches of carrots. Even that's different between the hippie moms and straight moms. The straight moms come out of Bartlett's carrying new grocery bags filled with neat even packages, and the hippie moms come out of the Co-op with crumpled fuzzy recycled bags leaking old loose lentils. We pile the groceries into the back of the van, checking on the sly to see if they got us any plums or sesame candies or even seaweed chips. As we leave, the van is full of scruffy arguing kids and dusty heat that smells like engine oil. In the front seat are just two clouds of hair with noses poking out, Susan and Helene.

At Matt and Melena and Andrew's house the moms are busy in the kitchen making brown rice and aduki beans, and Melena is set to grinding sesame seeds for gomasio. Remember to work in a counterclockwise motion to properly release the energy of the food, Helene warns, and leans over Melena to guide her arms the right way. Melena wrinkles her nose and looks sideways at Helene. Sourpuss, Helene says. I have to make tea and sprouted wheat toast for everyone. Andrew has to wipe old crumbs off the table and shake out the cushions, which makes him start arguing with Haud and Matt because they're wrestling on the cushions, rolling over them and around on the floor. Matt and Melena and Andrew's house is just like ours, which is another reason I like them. Everyone has to share rooms and beds, and their beds are just futons on the floor. The same dumb mandalas and hippie books: *Black Elk Speaks* and *Diet for a Small Planet* and *The Tibetan Book of the Dead*.

While we wait for dinner we listen to Beatles records and take turns being the band. Even Andrew plays. You kids are making waaaay too much noise, mellow out, Helene says, and we go outside but it's too hot. On the back porch Melena and I compare arm hairs and brush each other's hair and brush Jude's hair and Ki's hair, and then we braid weeds into Ki's hair. Matt and Haud chase grasshoppers and Jude climbs very carefully and slowly in and out of a broken wagon, sitting for long moments in the wagon doing nothing, his face tilted sideways and up toward the sky. Andrew reads on a saggy couch in the shade, swatting absently at flies.

At supper we make eyes at each other about the beans when the moms aren't looking, and we kick each other under the table and concentrate hard on making our chopsticks work, sneaking sideways glances to see who does better. Later, we see *Yellow Submarine* at the tin-can-lying-on-its-side movie theater, which I actually don't like because it doesn't make any sense, but I like the short Cat Stevens movie that comes on first. In the van going home in the dark we sing a Cat Stevens song that was in the movie, "Banapple Gas," and then "Yellow Submarine," the moms singing too. Melena gives me a meaningful look when Susan is pulling into the yard to drop off me and Haud and Helene and Ki, and I remember to ask Helene, Can we please go to the Free School, to Monte Rio Alternative School too, like Matt and Melena and Andrew? We'll see, Helene says, and I fall asleep thinking up names for the tiny fairy, like Thumbelina, who is my imaginary friend, and names for the bird she rides around on.

Chapter 5

We Are the Macroteam

Maybe my karma was good or something because guess what? We got to go to the Free School. Helene went to go see it and came home with almost new red tennies for me from the free box and a big box of blocks for Haud from the Salvation Army and said, No more straight school for my Buddha babies. No one will put any trips on you at the Free School. The groovy sisters and radical brothers there are in the process of throwing off the bourgeois yoke. No one asked me for your Social Security numbers or my previous addresses. But the Free School bus doesn't come out this far, so you're going to have to hitchhike to the bridge and walk from there. Me and Susan decided her kids will hitch with you. She can drive you guys sometimes and then sometimes she'll drop her kids here and then you can all hitch together.

So we started going to the Free School and this was a great time, when every day had a regularness and sameness. I would wake up and make lunches for us while Haud splashed around in the bathroom and then played with Ki on the rug. If Helene woke up she would have a cup of coffee in bed and holler from her bed not to put too much oil in the rice I fried for breakfast or too much miso on the tofu sandwiches I was making for lunch. If she didn't wake up I put as much oil in the rice or miso in the sandwiches as I wanted. The light coming through the windows would be first a dirty dark gray and then a dirty light gray, and Helene would be just a hump under the covers when we passed her dark bedroom on our way out. When Susan honked, we grabbed our lunch bags and ran to the car idling on the road, smoke coming from the rumbling tailpipe and Donovan playing on the radio. Or Andrew would toss a pebble at the side of the house if the kids had all walked to our house, and we would go single-file along the side of the road with our thumbs out until someone stopped for us. The mist over the tops of the trees made the forest seem quieter and made our breath steam in the air and water droplets bead on our sweaters. Even while the days were still hot the mornings would be cool and quiet like this, the forest waiting for us to wake it up. We kids tromping down the road to school together made a noise that told the forest we were there, instead of before when just Haud and I walked to the bus together and the forest seemed to be shushing us.

This was the first time ever that I went to school every day, the first time my life went in a straight line. Well, for a while it did, and I didn't think to wonder how long it would last. I liked this time, with Melena walking next to me and Haud scampering up ahead neighing like a horse and Andrew reading while he walked and Matt walking backwards with his thumb out. I felt, I tried to find the word, *safe*, somewhere that I belonged. A light misty rain fell every morning, not enough to make us wet but enough to drape a silvery beaded curtain over the rhododendrons and Queen Anne's lace and willows. In the afternoons when we walked back from school it would be hot again and we'd eat handfuls of dusty blackberries right from the road, red crunchy sour ones and dark ripe ones that fell apart when we picked them. Patient oaks gave us some shade while we waited for people to give us rides, and the foxgloves and grape ivy and tall furry mulleins wilted and grasshoppers whirred.

The Free School sits off the road going south out of town and right by the creek. It has a huge mural painted on the side of the building facing the road, a mural of dolphins and whales that says Monte Rio Alternative School. It has its own gym and its own library and a bunch of little classrooms with big windows and a big playground in the back with a jungle gym and a merry-go-round and hopscotch and a track for track and field. There's a basement for wood shop and ceramics and batik and tie-dye projects. Even swing sets and a sandbox. The classrooms all have round tables with chairs all around them instead of desks by themselves. There are shelves full of books and games and toys and junk, and house plants and an aquarium. There are rugs and cushions and smooshy beanbag chairs to sink down and read in.

The school has maybe thirty or forty kids, from five- and six-year-olds up to teenagers. On the first day I go there, I find out that Scott and Cynthia go there, too. Scott is in one of the classrooms when I come in and says, Hey Clane Train Clane Train going down the track clickety CLACK, which I don't mind.

What are you doing? I ask. Math, he says. Do you have to do math? No, you can do anything you want. Cynthia is in the gym with other kids and the drama and dance teacher in a big circle while a record player in the corner plays Crosby, Stills, and Nash. Welcome, sister, join us, the teacher says, We're doing improvisational movement therapy. All the teachers, but they're not called teachers, have long hair and wear tai chi pants and tie-dye like Helene. Some even have bare feet.

Just like Melena said, there aren't regular classes where you have to go to a certain room at a certain time. Instead there are things called discussion groups or forums or talk circles. A teacher will say, Gather round folks, it's time for a talk circle. In this discussion group we want a free flow of ideas in a nonhierarchical setting. No one is the authority here, we are all the authority here. The teachers will start off with a problem like, Does anyone here know what racism is? Does anyone here know California's history? We'll sit and sprawl and lie on the floor and cushions and in the beanbag chairs and listen and talk. California's history is the history of colonial oppression and genocide, a teacher will say. What is oppression? What is genocide? You don't have to raise your hand, just speak up. The Spaniards arrived to find native Californians, who they killed, and the Mexicans took it from the Spaniards, and the whites took it from the Mexicans, and everyone killed and oppressed the Indians, the teacher says.

The teachers invite us to the talk circles but we don't have to go if we absolutely don't want to, and they invite us to math if we want to, and if we want to we can just read all of the time, which is what I do for hours and hours. I plant pumpkin seeds in old milk cartons and set a piece of string in a glass of sugar water to make rock candy. I make kites and I do watercolors and I play capture the flag about a thousand times. No one ever says anything about the cosmic cats on my overalls and plenty of kids have strange names, Sunshine and Rainbow and Squirrel and Shiva and Rama.

There are things called workshops too. There is batik workshop. In batik workshop Haud dyes his hands blue and pretends he's one of the Blue Meanies from *Yellow Submarine*. There is ceramics, where I make wobbly clay pots on a wheel and a statue of a mermaid. Haud makes an ashtray with a pot leaf drawn in it and a bunch of snails clumped together and calls it "Snails Going to Town." There is wood shop, and I make a little shelf that goes by my bed for my bottle of rose water and my tea set. Haud pretends he is battling giant ants with a propane torch, going, Die die! and making shrieking sounds and singeing things until a teacher catches him and says, Let's talk about these antisocial fantasies, Haud.

One day everyone paints a mural on the side of the school. Grownups and teachers trace outlines and scenery on the wall in chalk, mix buckets of paint, and tie smocks around the little kids, who are busy splattering themselves and everything else but the mural in paint. Kids stand against the wall holding still in different positions while others trace around them, and then they fill in the shapes. Everyone gets a brush and a smock and a rag tucked into a pocket. I add jungle vines and flowers around the kid shapes. Someone paints a rainbow and someone paints a mountain covered in snow and someone paints a dragon. It looks confused but still nice when it's finished, late in the day, and everyone is spotted and smudged with paint.

A theater troupe comes to the school and teaches everyone how to be mimes and make human pyramids. With everyone sitting on the floor in front of him, this dude talks to us. His name is Peter, Peter Coyote. He says, Okay, what did everyone have for breakfast? Oatmeal, someone says, and the man draws a picture of oats growing. He says, Where does the oatmeal go? In your stomach, we say, and he draws a picture of someone eating. Then where does the oatmeal go? It's a turd inside you, he says, and we all shriek. Where does the turd go? He draws a picture of a turd in a toilet and we shriek again. Then where does the turd go? It goes into the sea when you flush the toilet. Is this a good thing? No. What can we all do about it? he asks. We need to develop environmental awareness and stewardship of this earth. After this there is a big project where we make a whale as big as two cars out of chicken wire and papier mâché. We put it on a trailer thingy and drag it through the streets chanting, Save the gray, save the blue, save the humpback and killer too, save the whales oh save the whales, the time is right, so do it now.

Later on, early in the fall there is Gold Rush Days. We have talk circles and learn about the gold rush in California, when everyone came to California when gold was discovered here in the 1840s. Miners came from everywhere to rape the land, out of greed for gold and lust for profits. The miners turned Chinese people into slaves because of this greed, and killed each other and stole each other's gold. All week we build old-time jails and stores and banks and saloons out of cardboard, a miniature California gold-rush town. Then early one morning before the kids get to school the teachers hide pieces of white gravel all over the school grounds without saying anything, and then someone shouts Gold Rush! Gold in the hills! and we all run screaming outside to look for the gold. Little kids roll over each other fighting in the dirt to get each other's gold, and bigger kids shove little kids out of the way until they run off crying and tell some teachers. The teachers watch in shock and then rush around helpless to do anything as packs of kids tear each other's shirts and pull hair and push each other down. As soon as someone finds gold, the nearest kids pounce on the kids who find it and take it, until there's no more gold to be found and everyone is streaked in dirt and tears, the big kids with bulging pockets and the little kids hiccuping sobs and covered in scratches, with leaves and twigs in their hair. All the big kids get thrown into jail by the teachers, yelling and protesting, and some of their gold is taken away and given to some of the little kids who didn't get any. Then we have a meeting about fairness and sharing and community. Then everyone trades their gold for juice and cookies and candy at the saloon. Kids who cheated or fought are sent back to jail by other kids with sheriff stars pinned to their shirts. Groups of kids gloat over their riches or snuffle their tears, mouths full of cookies. Gold Rush Days are great.

Something is always happening at the Free School. We go on field trips to see movies, *Close Encounters of the Third Kind*, to Sebastopol to see apple orchards, to a place in Santa Rosa where you can see how the earliest California Indians and rancheros lived. At Halloween there's going to be a pumpkin carving contest.

I have been doing my best not to say much about school so Helene won't come there and ruin it, but she hears about the pumpkin carving contest. She dresses Ki up like a fairy princess in a white dress and flowers in her hair and paints mandalas on her cheeks and she comes to school. I brought you paints for your pumpkin, Clanie, she says, so you can make it really cosmic and stoney. She paints a goddess and pot leaves in silver on my pumpkin, without asking! Our pumpkin is the weirdest one in the contest and I think to myself that for sure someone is going to say something but no one does. I go off to sulk in a corner because she ruined my pumpkin.

Cynthia comes and plops down on the floor beside me and gives me some raisins she won for her costume, which is

Pocahontas. Your mom's hair is cool, Cynthia says. Want to come to my house and spend the night? When I ask her Helene shrugs and says, Knock yourself out, but no shitfood, so I go home with them when their mom comes and we watch TV and eat peanut butter and banana sandwiches. Since they're on whole wheat bread that means they're not shitfood. You can have bananas, I'm sure, can't you? Cynthia's mom says skeptically, like no one could have a fit about bananas, not knowing that Helene would for sure have a fit about bananas, which I wisely stay quiet about. I've never seen TV before and it's amazing, a Charlie Brown Halloween special, and only the chance to kiss with Scott on the porch is enough to tear me away. We sit on the couch on the porch, which leans way out over the hill because it's on stilts on a hill, and we hold hands, only Cynthia comes too, which I'm not mad about, actually glad, because Scott's all, Do you want to be on top or on bottom? and I'm all, I don't think that's how you kiss.

After this it's hard for me to go back to my house except that at Cynthia's I missed Ki and maybe Haud. Our house seems darker than before and I notice the crumbs on the floor and the dirty dishes and the droopy houseplants. I spend the next two nights at Matt and Melena and Andrew's house, except now I miss Ki for real and cry into my pillow a tiny bit because I feel confused. I don't want to live with Helene anymore, I decide, but then I think, Who's going to take care of Ki? She's always eating things off the sidewalk and falling into mud puddles and once she even fell face first into a bowl of cereal when she tripped on a rug. Back at Helene's I'm thinking about this, tucked away on the top shelf of the closet, and I'm thinking how it would be if me and Ki were identical twins and had matching outfits, and I start planning a birthday party for us with cake and strawberry ice cream. Helene stands outside the closet looking up at me going, I know you're in there thinking about shitfood, Clane. I thought if you went to a Free School you'd stop the head trips about shitfood. They're not putting you on head trips about school, are you? Offering you nutrition information, and she screws up her face when she says nutrition information. I'm going to go to the school and talk to the sisters and brothers about having macrobiotic lunches, she says, and marches off to do tarot. The next time Ki tries to eat something off the sidewalk, a piece of dried-up carrot, and she looks all guilty and sad when I catch her and say, No, Ki, bad, bad, I think, Your head trips are the worst of all, Helene. Yours is the head trip, your kids eat food out of garbage cans and off the sidewalk because of your head trips.

For Thanksgiving there is a community potluck at the school and we bring a big pot of brown rice. There is a turkey made out of wheat gluten and a turkey made out of soybeans. There's baked squash and miso sauce and homemade bread, and someone brings lasagna. Helene catches me trying to get some lasagna and she grabs me by the elbow and lectures the lady who brought it. But it's vegetarian, the lady says, bewildered. Cheese has rennet in it, Helene says. Do you know what rennet is?

Helene asks. Rennet is the lining of cow stomachs. While she is lecturing the lady, the lady's face all rapt and interested now, talking about digestion and balance and blocked energy flows and how the lady can clear up her skin just like that on a brown rice diet, I sneak a piece of carrot cake and give some to Ki, and me and Melena sneak another piece and eat it in the closet, laughing.

Hanukkah is a bummer, a total bummer. Matt and Melena and Andrew and Jude and Susan all go to San Francisco to light the menorah at the Jewish temple. I don't know what a Menorah celebration is but I'm painfully jealous anyway, and then lonely without them. There isn't any school for days and days and Haud and I wander around under the great dark dank trees playing ghosts and pirates, hiding in huge old stumps and looking for clues to a secret code that I know, after all, isn't really there. Me and Haud make paper chains and strings of popcorn but Helene says, No Christmas tree unless it's living, no way are we going to chop down a defenseless little tree. Haud goes into the forest behind our house and digs one up and sticks it into a bucket of dirt. But I didn't kill it, he whines, covered in dirt and twigs and pine needles. We don't have a celebration or anything, we just eat some rice and then I read and we go to bed. But in the morning there's a paint set for me and a wooden car for Haud and puzzles for Ki.

Later on when Matt and Melena and Andrew come backm we're playing at their house. We're reading comic books and listening to the Beatles. Matt has a yellow towel tied around his neck and plays he's Superboy. Andrew looks up from a book and says all of a sudden, We should have our own team like the Superfriends. We all stop and look at him because when he talks, which is almost never, we know it's serious. We could all wear different costumes, I say. And have weapons, says Haud. I'll have a nuclear stun ray powered by a portable battery pack, he says, and Andrew says it's noo-clear not noo-kuh-ler. We all put down what we're doing and start dancing around shouting different ideas. I'm Light Girl and I'll have a super high-powered flashlight to blind the enemy. Melena can be Color Girl and she'll distract the enemy by throwing clouds of poison confetti. I'm Karate Boy, Matt says, chopping the air with his arms and going hi-yah hi-yah. What are we called? The Macroteam, Andrew decides, We're the Macroteam like for macrobiotic. We'll make a secret network of tunnels through the blackberry bushes so we can go anywhere in town fast and invisible. Who are our enemies? We stop a minute, no one can figure out who the enemy is, and we finally decide it's anyone who picks on us. The week school starts back Matt gets beat at tether ball and Scott makes fun of him, so Matt yells, Macroteam! and jumps around and does kicks and twirls and chops the air going hi-yah hi-yah hi-yah. Suddenly Haud and Melena are right there too and we all take defensive stances around Matt. Scott looks at us like, You weirdos, and stalks away.

Lunchtime. Me and Melena and Matt and Haud get our lunches from the cloakroom. I have a thermos of rice and miso soup which is like two weeks old. Melena says, Pour it down the drain, in the girls' bathroom, I'll give you half my sandwich. Matt is stuffing cookies fast as he can into his mouth, and Haud notices and Melena too and they say, Where'd you get the cookies? and Matt won't say. The next day Melena has an orange, which she's not supposed to, and Matt has a peanut butter sandwich on white bread, which he's definitely not supposed to, and even though we always eat our lunch on the merry-go-round they want to go eat down by the creek. I go because I want some of Matt's sandwich. Next day we all go down to the creek again and this time Melena has little cheeses wrapped in foil, the ones with the smiling cow on them, and Matt has potato chips. Where'd you get this? I breathe. We'll show you tomorrow, Matt says.

Just before lunch next day Matt says quietly in my ear, Macroteam meets in the cloakroom in five minutes. Melena tells Haud and we all slip into the cloakroom when we're alone in the hall. We stand there looking at each other for a minute, breathing hard. Matt reaches into one of the lunch bags the kids all put on shelves near their jackets and coats. We each open a bag and quick look in and grab what looks good and close the bag back up and then run out of the cloakroom along the hall out the back door through a hole in the fence down a path to the creek. I've got a peanut butter and jelly sandwich, Haud has animal crackers, Matt has celery and peanut butter. Melena has cheeses again. We do it again the next day. Hiding in the bushes by the creek we compare the food we stole and trade and argue.

Friday morning we're finked out. I see a clump of teachers talking quietly with concerned looks on their faces in the hall. One of them looks at me and I look him square in the eye as I walk past and put my bag of tofu sandwiches in the cloakroom. I sit down by the door and take off one of my shoes and pretend I'm getting rocks out of it while gently easing the door open a crack and listening. I hear someone saying, She's not supposed to eat sugar or white bread, and someone else is saying, They were raiding lunch bags from the cloakroom, and someone else is saying, We'll have to have a group discussion. I know they're talking about Melena and not me because I would never crack, I'd never fink out, but my stomach does cold flip-flops and my heart is pounding and I feel really really really bad. It didn't seem like such a big deal at the time. It was so easy and it didn't seem wrong, but all day it's what everyone talks about, all the kids and grownups too.

There's no group discussion but when I find Matt he's snuffling snotty tears though his swollen nose and Melena's eyes are red and her face is all white. We sit on the merry-go-round at lunch, not eating, swinging our feet, Melena wiping her eyes with her sleeves, Matt wiping his nose on his sleeves. I don't know which is worse, that they got finked out or that there's no more little cheeses and animal crackers. I feel bad that they got caught but not me, but not bad enough to confess that I did it too. I pat Melena's back and her skinny bones stick up through her shirt and she's hunched over, still crying.

After this the Macroteam sort of goes nuts. I steal apples and carob bars and handfuls of granola from the Co-op on my way home from school. Haud waits near where the straight kids get on the bus every morning for their school and pushes them down and grabs their lunches and runs off. The four of us watch houses to see which ones are empty for the winter, and we jiggle open windows or break them to get in and steal food and eat it down by the river. We eat boxes of stale saltines and drink bottles of pancake syrup, we take bags of sugar, cans of sardines. One time Haud and Matt take a whole case of Chef Boy-Ar-Dee ravioli, but no one has a can opener, so after banging the cans on rocks for a while we give up.

Chapter 6

Yippie the Hippie Caravan Is Off

Throughout early spring it rains all the time, it rains and rains and rains. No one wants to hitchhike to school in the rain so we skip a lot. Sometimes Susan drives us. Helene won't drive at all and anyway she doesn't have a car. We used to have a truck that we named Butterfly or sometimes Flutterby, but something happened to it, I don't know what. Our house seems darker and colder than even before and it smells like mildewy carpet. I walk to the library in the rain and I ask Helene for a raincoat and she say,s You don't want to be wrapped up in plastic, wear one of your wool sweaters, wool is very water-resistant. But it smells like wet dog, I say, and she sighs heavily. Sometimes I read in the big chair under a lamp all day, *The Voyage of the Dawn Treader* and *The Silver Chair* and *Beezus and Ramona* and *The Secret Garden*.

The river swells up and turns brown and runs fast. It gets to near our porch even. I watch the river through the screen door and think about this book I read about a girl in Kansas during the Depression. I feel like I'm in a Depression, except that I'm stuck shivering in a musty damp redwood forest instead of sweltering through a drought in Kansas. In the book the girl is poor and her family has to move a lot to find work and they really want to find a home to settle down in, but Helene never wants to stay anywhere and she doesn't care that we're poor and she doesn't want to find work. And in the book, the girl loves her family and they always hug, but I never hug Helene and I'm not sure I love her. She's not lovey, she's not mom-ey. She doesn't have a mom feel and she for sure doesn't set out a plate of cookies and a glass of milk for me when I get home from school.

Things get worse. Way worse, because we have lice. Susan comes over one day to tell Helene that the kids have lice and she better check us for lice too. Helene sits me on the floor in front of the sofa and paws through my hair saying, Hold still dammit, I think I found something. She's pulling my hair, which is knotty and tangly, and she finds a louse and shows me and I shiver with the grossness of it. The louse looks like a little crab. Haud has them too and so does Ki. We take a trip to Bartlett's to buy Kwell, which is a de-louser, and a nit comb. The back of the Kwell box says the hair must be combed carefully for nits, which are lice eggs, and can hatch even after the Kwell kills the lice.

Going into Bartlett's I notice how the way we look is so different from everything around us. It's Helene's layers of skirts over pants and the rings on her toes, and our long ratty hair and homemade clothes, but it's more than that. Other people in Bartlett's, other kids and moms and dads, have the same colors and shades, they look like what's in the store, brighter-than-real colors, things that are new and gleaming. The way the rows of cans and boxes and bags have a pattern of sameness and regularity, the people do too. The way the fluorescent light in the store bounces off the neat rows of cereal boxes and candy bars and juice bottles is the same way the light reflects from the people's shiny watches and belt buckles and earrings and plastic purses and polyester pants. Not us. We suck light from the air. We stand out from the pattern like a cloud of funk.

We spend the whole day in the bathroom, one after the other being de-loused and then de-loused again and then nit-picked. None of us kids have ever been so clean or had our hair so untangled. With Susan and her kids, who also get de-loused, we make a trip to the laundromat to wash all of the bedding and all our clothes. In the rain, everyone drags bag after bag of stuff to Susan's car and then into the laundromat and into washers and then dryers. Susan buys seven new bandanas and tells us we have to wear the bandanas until we're sure no one has lice anymore. The bandanas will keep the lice from jumping onto other people's heads, she tells us.

She drives us to school the next day, a carload of miserable damp kids all wearing blue and red bandanas. The grownups at school call a discussion group where we talk about lice and how you get lice from contact with other things or people that carry lice. No one is pointing any fingers or doing any blaming here, the dance and drama teacher says, It's not important how the lice got into our school, the ceramics lady says, and everyone looks at the five of us sitting hunched and scowling in our bandanas. If you think you might have lice or are afraid you're going to get lice, wear a scarf or a hat. We scowl harder.

Melena's face is pinched so tight her lips are white, and Haud is glowering so fiercely his eyebrows are drawn together in a single dark line across the top of his face. I stare into nothing and try to get a look of innocence on my face, like Who, me? Andrew crosses his arms and flares his nostrils and looks up at the ceiling. Matt absently and sadly wipes his nose on his sleeve.

It rains and rains more and the river rises even higher. It comes right to the porch, swirling under the wooden floorboards in little whirlpools that carry twigs and leaves and feathers and weeds and pinecones and fir needles. The three of us kids crouch on the porch watching for water snakes and swiping things out of the muddy drift. The water is seeping under the door soon and the carpet is squishing and we're going to stay in Susan's school bus for a while. Susan's house is flooded out too. Nine of us in the bus, all damp and smelling like wet dog, but us kids are happy and goofy because it's an adventure and Helene doesn't care that we're flooded out of our house because she says we owe the landlord three months rent and we were going to be evicted soon anyway. Only Susan is upset. Helene tells her, Just get stoned, lady, everything looks better with hemp. Dope will get you through times of no money better than money will get you through times of no dope, she says, huffing a big cloud of pot smoke, passing the roach to Susan. No left turn on stoned, she says, cackling laughter.

The moms decide we're going to drive the bus down to San Francisco. Helene says she can score a little money off Ki's grandmother and off mine and Haud's grandmother. I didn't know we had a grandmother. We'll go see Stash and Puma, Helene says. Maybe we can crash at their pad for a while.

We have to leave all our toys, which is really just our blocks and paint set and a jump rope, at school. Andrew has to give up his record player and the Beatles and Jefferson Airplane albums, Matt has to give up his skateboard, there's not room on the bus. Can we have our stuff back later? we say anxiously, and Helene says who knows what the future holds, yippie, the hippie caravan is off. In the endless rain, we drag the last few bags of stuff onto the bus and put the big stuff on top tied down and covered with tarps. Susan sits in the driver's seat looking small against the huge steering wheel and grinds the gears a little getting started. The wheels spin in the wet gravel and mud of the driveway and all the kids chant, Power to the bus, power to the bus, power to the bus, and with a growl and then a lurch we're up over the lip of the drive and down the road, cheering.

We drive slow on the narrow wet road and branches slap us going past and the tires make a sucking sound on the asphalt. Matt and Haud horse around in the aisle, Andrew reads a comic book. Melena holds Jude and I hold Ki, and Helene sits on a seat just behind Susan and they talk about the benevolence of Shiva and the negative death trip of the American presidency. After a while Ki is asleep and drooling a little, her face pressed up against the window, and a little later all of us kids are asleep, lulled by the low growl of the engine in the warm steamy bus.

We wake up a little later, stretching and looking around bleary-eyed, when the air gets cooler because we're closer to the bay. We pass Sausalito and the houseboats rocking on the flat gray bay. We go slow up the big hill before the Rainbow Tunnel, the engine straining a little and lurching when Susan has to go to a lower gear. We go through the Rainbow Tunnel holding our breaths for luck and then taking big whoops of air scrubbed clean by rain. The slopes of the headlands just before the Golden Gate bridge are covered in fennel and french-fry plants and the peculiar knotty hairy plants that grow near salt air and cold seas, and the air has its own certain smell here, the fennel and something sharp like lemon but earthy like clay and acrid like manzanita and yarrow. Then we're on the Golden Gate Bridge, elegant and airy, arching up like a fairy castle, and then we're passing the Presidio and the smell of eucalyptus fills the bus, and this is San Francisco to me. This smell of the eucalyptus and the way the mist floats over the tops of the trees in the Avenues.

Susan parks the bus in the Avenues and we make a plan to meet back here. Circle the wagons, Helene says, we're in the city now. I've got to do some heavy hustling, Helene says, and then we'll meet in a few days. She packs one of her hippie bags with some clothes and junk and the I Ching and puts on her slippers and picks up Ki and steps off the bus, me and Haud following. We walk down the Avenues past the cracker-box houses that all look the same until we find a parking lot where she tells us to pee and she finds a phone booth and calls Lynn. Little old Chinese ladies look at us, carrying plastic shopping bags and pink cake boxes and scurrying fast like little bent-over stick ladies.

Lynn is Ki's grandmother, Bruce's mother, and she lives here in the Avenues in one of the little boxy houses with a fake balcony and a little front yard full of gravel and shrubs trimmed into squares. Her house is crammed full of grandmother stuff, glass animals and china flowers and fake fruit in jeweled bowls. You can't move without knocking something and we kids are shy and quiet, Ki looking around with big round eyes. There's little fuzzy fake deer and crystal swans and embroidered pillows and thick carpet everywhere, even a plushy toilet-seat cover.

We're going to spend the night with Lynn. She's little and fake blond, in a matching pink pantsuit with furry slippers. She makes a lot of kissy fussy sounds over us and shows me little rose-shaped soaps in the bathroom and says I can use them, and lets me open all her bottles of lotions and perfumes and says I can try them all. You smell like a Turkish brothel, Helene says. Lynn lets Haud turn on the record player and the TV but there's only football on. She gives me a ball and jacks and shows me how to play on the kitchen floor while she and Helene talk about wheat-free diets and lactose intolerance. Lynn is the only straight person I know who will go on and on with Helene about food without getting mad, because she has a lot of food allergies and eats weird food too, only not as weird as us of course. She gives Ki a doll called Little Baby Live, which cries and smacks its lips when you squeeze it, and you can feed it food that comes in little packets with a tiny spoon. You can change its diapers. Ki shakes the doll around but doesn't really know what to do with it, she's only two and a half and she's never had a plastic doll before.

Me and Haud share a big bed in the guest room that has sheets folded perfectly over a fuzzy pink blanket and two pillows placed exactly even at the top of the bed. I'm not used to sheets, they make a lot of noise and I'm afraid to move because I don't want to mess up the perfect bed and it's too hot under all those covers and I'm not used to the streetlight shining outside the window like a fake moon or the sound of cars going by all night. I'm homesick for something but I don't know what.

I guess Lynn gives Helene money. We leave the next morning with more kissy sounds and lots of hugging. Also in the Avenues lives Helene's mother, Ethel, mine and Haud's grandmother. Helene says Ethel is straight and always will be. By straight she means someone who eats donuts and lives in a nice house and wears clothes that match and shoes with socks and doesn't smoke pot. Can't teach that dog new tricks, Helene says. We might as well get this over with. She says, We always have a hard time at Ethel's because once Haud shat on her floor. I don't remember that, I say, and she says, You were too young. Not even three. We take a bus to Ethel's, another little box of a house, this one with a yard of redwood chips and a bush with no flowers and no smell. Ethel has no smell and her house has no smell and her hair has no color and her eyes are watery blue and bugged out behind thick glasses. She's older than Lynn and it seems to me like she doesn't recognize us, just sits in a flowery chair holding a little dog, Baby, on her lap. Baby has long hair pulled up into ponytails behind her ears and tied with little pink bows. Ethel has the same kind of fake fruit as Lynn, and fake flowers and fake ivy hanging from the ceiling, which has gold sparkles on it. She offers us Safeway-brand cola and Sno-Balls which, duh, Helene won't let us have, which seems to mystify Ethel, but she doesn't say anything, just goes back to her chair and back to petting Baby. I guess she gives money to Helene too. Maybe just to get rid of her.

We haven't had anything to eat because Helene wouldn't let us have anything that Lynn or Ethel offered, even though Lynn is a vegetarian. Hungry and whining, we wait for another bus and get on it while as usual people look at us funny, especially two little black kids hanging over the back of the seat in front of us. They look at us a long time without blinking while the bus lurches. I look at the little girl, maybe five or six, and she looks at me, and she screws up her face in a great big smile and I want so bad to touch her little chocolate-colored hands hanging onto the seat. We're going to see Stash in the Haight.

Stash and her old man, Easy, and her kids Dana and Puma live two or three stories up in a fancy but peeling building with a narrow staircase and dust and dog hairs on the stairs. Stash has a crazy mane of hair like Helene's and they hug each other going, Hey sister, hey magical sister. I tried to call you again and again but all I got was a busy signal, Helene says. Yeah, we've got the phone off the hook because Easy needs to sleep. He's dope sick, he's trying to kick heroin. Right away they get into a discussion about how a macrobiotic diet will help him. Dana and Puma take me and Haud into their room to play, and we have to go through the room where Easy is sleeping, which smells like something animal. Dana lets me try on her fancy clothes and Puma and Haud scowl at each other. Puma is fat and has piggy eyes and breathes loudly through his mouth. We stay all afternoon, Stash braiding dreadlocks into Helene's hair while Dana teaches me crochet at the kitchen table and Puma and Haud lean over the back porch, watching their spit fall three stories down and seeing who can make the longest chain of spit. Ki plays with some string and falls asleep under a chair until we wake her up because we're going to the Good Karma Cafe.

The Good Karma Cafe is on Dolores near the park and has a huge lotus flower painted on the front wall. Inside it smells delicious, like curry and rice pudding, which Helene might let us have but she'll grumble about the honey in it, so is the rice pudding worth the grumbling? The cafe is full of hippies. The warm fragrant dark is lit by candles and there are strings of beads hanging on all the doors and Indian-print cloth on the walls. I have the huge wonderful feeling of having something good to eat from a pretty plate with flowers on it and a fork, not chopsticks, and a nice waitress who doesn't look at us weird when Helene asks is the brown rice organic.

Afterwards we sit on a blanket in the park and Helene and Stash talk. They talk about Easy going to jail and about how

Helene almost went to jail for shoplifting. The pigs are always hassling me, she says. Almost went to jail for stealing from the stealers, had my pants stuffed full of winter socks for the kids. That's all, just socks. It's the owners who are owned, Helene says. All property is theft. Try taking ginseng to keep the cops away, Stash says. Chew on a piece of ginseng root, it lengthens your alpha waves and this reduces paranoia. Stash laughs. You kids have really grown up, she says. The last time I saw you, Bruce had you singing and playing maracas in Chinatown while he played guitar for spare change. I scowl. Haud scowls. He played those Neil Young songs and you kids had to sing about the Kent State killings. She laughs again. So where's Bruce now? Now Helene scowls. Haud and Puma pull each other's hair and me and Dana make daisy chains for Ki's hair, only she tries to eat the daisies and Helene says, Don't, there's probably dog piss on every square inch of this park. It's chilly and spitting rain on us, which beads up on the blanket and our wool sweaters. The long grassy green slope of the park stretches up before us, with just the tops of some palm trees visible at the high end. I love San Francisco, even though it's always foggy like this. We have to get back to the bus before it gets dark, Helene says. Maybe we can go see a movie. Star Wars? Haud says hopefully. Akira Kurosawa, Helene says. *Seven Samurai.* You kids will love that one.

Chapter 7

The Regularness and Sameness Ended

That was the last I saw of San Francisco for a very long time. We stood in the lobby of a big department store while Helene was busy stealing things for us, tennies and socks and small stuff she could stick in her pants or the sleeves of her sweater, and I was waiting for her and listening to the sounds of the city. Shoes on the marble floor and the rustle of bodies, shopping bags crackling and rustling, briefcases creaking, doors opening and closing, taxis honking and squealing and braking, big truck brakes squeaking and their heavy doors clanging open and closed, jackhammers, traffic moving in rushed bursts. I was holding Ki's hand, and Haud was skipping across the floor to make his shoes squeak. There was the sound of a cable car moving past, the sound of police and fire sirens, everything moving quickly and jangling. I was listening to the buses moving along their electric lines with sighs and belches, to the layers of sound the city makes, and I was thinking, This is the city and I am in it. Here is me listening to the city as it moves around me.

I did that, listened to the city as it moved around me like a galaxy wheeling around one small moonfaced me, and then I didn't see a city for a long time. Helene made another one of her decisions that I never understood and just had to follow. She decided we were going to not live in houses anymore, no more rent, no more landlords. No one can really own the land, she said. The land abides and we live on it and we will live by the grace of God.

So we moved into the forest and we lived there a long time, long enough for me to turn twelve. We lived sometimes in campgrounds with picnic tables and sometimes just in open fields and sometimes under redwoods and once at the beach in a house made out of driftwood. We lived a while on an abandoned ranch, once by a river, once deep in a forest used for logging, with gargantuan stumps torn out of the earth that left holes so big we used one for a swimming pool after a long rain. Susan and Matt and Melena and Andrew and Jude came with us. I never saw the house by the river in Monte Rio again. What we needed of our things we'd taken on the bus when it started to rain, and we just took it all with us when we became enchanted forest people. We had just our clothes and bedding and cooking stuff. Mom's bag of embroidery, some books, kerosene lamps. My little tea set, I kept it as safe as I could the whole time. I don't know what happened to the school bus.

The first place we lived was a picnic table at a campsite by the river, somewhere near Monte Rio but far away from town. The table, an old scarred wooden one, was the kitchen, dining room, and living room. We had a little propane stove and a little canister of gas at the center. Piled nearby were our bowls and plates and mason jars of chopsticks and wooden spoons and

Chinese soupspoons and a few old bent forks. The kerosene lamp. Bags and jars of rice, millet, seaweed, sesame seeds, sunflower seeds, beans, a jar of tamari crusted down the sides with trails of old drips. A big jug of water, a ripped towel, a roll of toilet paper. Helene's embroidery bag, piles of coloring books and the I Ching with its cover bending and spotted with mildew. Scattered piles of things that were always a little dusty and damp and tattered. Under the table we had milk crates and cardboard boxes holding our pots and pans and the wok, the cardboard limp and trying to melt into the ground, sprigs of fir and pine needles and leaves always on everything.

Around the table we would cook and sit and talk, coloring and squabbling while we waited to eat, Helene or Susan reaching over and around us to stir the pots, lighting the lamp at dusk. Jude and Ki played under the table, Haud and Matt chased each other around it, while Andrew sat reading and absently picking his nose. There wasn't room for everyone at the table and if you got there too soon you had to sit forever to keep your spot, and no saving spots, we all agreed. If you were slow to get to the table you had to take your bowl and spoon and sit on a tree stump nearby or on the ground. Slow you blow, Matt would say. Snooze you lose, Andrew would say. I always heard that, all the times I lived with a lot of people that was what I heard if I was late to the table and there was no dinner left or last to choose a place to sleep and only got the scratchy blanket. If Helene and Susan forgot to yell at us we'd all be at the pot shoving and elbowing, saying, You're eating from my side, he got more than me, quit hogging, and someone always ended up sitting on the ground scowling and sulking.

Our bathroom, the washing our faces and brushing our teeth part, was the river. We crouched at the bank, shivering and splashing water on ourselves, getting our sleeves and cuffs damp, and only after being yelled at to do it by Susan. Helene didn't care if we washed up or not. We peed and pooed behind trees and clumps of bushes and then covered it with dirt and took the dirty toilet paper and burned it every now and then in a little campfire spot.

The bedroom was a big tarp spread on the ground at the base of some giant trees. We used our bags of clothes for pillows and we tucked our books under our sleeping bags. When it was cold and got dark early we would be in bed at dusk, reading by the light of the kerosene lamp, Helene tossing the I Ching and muttering to herself or embroidering.

Sleeping under the trees like that, I really hated redwoods because the ground around them was always damp and I had to look for snails and slugs and moths and spiders. That was the worst thing about living outside, the bugs. You always have to check for them in your bed and your clothes and your shoes and your bowl, and when you find one it's hard not to panic and flip out. Melena and I were always screeching and flinging something away, flapping our hands in the air and plucking at our tangly hair going, Ick yuck grooooooooss, Mooooooom there's a spider on me. Earwigs are the total absolute worst, they have those pinchers on their ass.

The best thing about living outside was no housecleaning. No sweeping the floor or wiping the counter or making the beds or straightening up. We washed our dishes in the river or sometimes just wiped them out.

The other bad thing about living outside was the rain. If it rained we had to cover everything on the table in sheets of plastic, and then we all huddled on our beds with another sheet of plastic over us, all squished close to stay warm, making up games and stories or just curled up together napping and dozing like a den of smelly little foxes.

At first we tried to keep going to school, but Susan mostly didn't have gas money and no one wanted to hitchhike because we were on a road no one ever drove down. It would take hours to get a ride and people would look at us so funny, a group of ragged forest creatures coming out of the bushes, no houses around. When we did make it to school it felt all different than before. I knew it was crazy that we lived outside, not crazy to me, I got used to it, but crazy-looking to someone else. They would ask, How do you go to the bathroom? Where do you keep your clothes? How do you take a bath? I would shrug and wander away or pretend to be really busy with something, not wanting to explain. I asked Helene once. I asked, Are we ever going to live in a house again? Are we ever going to have a bathroom? And she said you want a bathroom? Why, so you can piss in something white? It was like we just didn't belong anymore. School was a circle that we went farther and farther to the edges of, starting with the lunch stealing and the lice and then the living at a picnic table.

That first place we lived, the picnic table, it was winter and gray all the time. The sky stayed the same, low and dense. Us kids walked along the river, looking for pretty stones or frogs or snakes, pushing through the elderberry bushes and willows, wearing thick sweaters for the cold and being careful not to fall in the water. We walked along the road, the trees always whispering at us. We picked sorrel and clovers from the forest floor for their sour taste, checking for slug trails first. We scouted out hollow redwood stumps for a clubhouse and made up long complicated games about bands of pirates, forest fairies, animal spirits, and the walking trees called Ents from *Lord of the Rings*.

Sometimes it was lonesome, just the light of our kerosene lamp against the whole big blackness of the forest. At dusk the tips of the trees stood out stark like dark spires of an evil castle against the lighter gray of the sky and this made me feel scared and small and like we were the last people on earth, lost and wandering in a kingdom that went on forever. When we were all going to sleep and no one was making any noise, the wind moving through the foliage was like the forest shushing me. I was a cursed princess trapped in a lonely empty kingdom waiting to be rescued by a beautiful fairy godmother. My fairy godmother would take me to a pretty little house with pink gingerbread scrolls and lace curtains, where I would have a canopy bed, a real one, and my long-lost twin sister would be waiting for me with new clothes and strawberries and cream for breakfast. The fairy godmother would take me out of this indifferent forest, huddled under my blankets under the tall trees in the dark.

Luckily we didn't stay under the redwood trees forever. There was a field we lived in for a while, still near Monte Rio. Moving there, it was like the whole sky lightened up and a weight I hadn't known was there lifted off my shoulders. I don't know if it belonged to anyone, the field, but we were able to stay there for a long time without anyone telling us to move. It was near the highway, far enough so the cars couldn't see us, but close enough so that we heard them and this made me feel like we weren't in the middle of nowhere. The field was circled by a dirt road and by oak and manzanita and elm trees, plus other scrubby trees I didn't know the names of but liked way better than redwoods. It was full of tall weeds that caught the morning dew with their fuzzy leaves, mullein and burdock and vetch, and which glistened like upside-down chandeliers in morning sunlight. Scotch broom and wild morning glories and Indian paintbrush, each of which had its own smell and their smell all together made up another smell. I like flowers best but I like weeds too, especially in the morning when the sun warms them and they give off that weedy wild smell, almost like honey but really a smell I can't name for sure.

In the field a circle of stones was our fire for cooking,, and this was the kitchen. We pulled logs from dead trees near the fire and laid down some scraps of carpet samples that Susan scored from a department store going out of business in Guerneville, and this was the dining room and the living room. We had the milk crates and now some orange crates. The ground was flatter and drier than the forest, and over time we beat the grass and weeds down flat all around the cook fire and in a path to our beds under the oak trees and in a path to the dirt road and in a crisscross of smaller paths all across the field. We could watch the stars when we fell asleep, and I got to really like this, watching for airplanes, falling stars, and satellites which we argued whether they were UFOs or not.

In the field we woke up early because the birds would start to sing just before the sun hit the tops of the distant trees. I would lie in my sleeping bag on my back with the covers pulled up to my nose, looking for the morning star, watching the mist moving off the trees. Before the sun came up there was always a fine mist of dew covering everything, the bushes and trees and weeds and even our blankets and hair. Not enough to be wet, not rain, just damp and only until the sun was up. It smelled good, the early morning air, and I would lie still, awake before anyone else, watching them wake up bit by bit. Ki and Jude always slept like little logs, Ki with her rump up in the air, Jude always all the way down in the covers. Matt and Haud slept with their sleeping bags in wild lumpy messes, crooked on the ground after rolling off the tarp, Andrew always straight and dignified even in sleep because he was older and more serious than us. Melena slept on her stomach all curled up, and Helene and Susan were always just clouds of hair, sometimes full of twigs or moss or leaves.

One or another of us would start to stir and make noise, yawning or mumbling or whispering to each other, reaching for clothes bags to drag a sweater or socks into the covers to warm up and then worming into our clothes without letting the cold morning air in. We pulled twigs and leaves and moss from our hair and rubbed our eyes and shivered as we got out of our sleeping bags to scurry, hunched and chilly, behind the trees to pee. Someone would be sent, complaining, to get twigs and firewood. Haud hopping around on one foot trying to get a shoe on, Melena asking sleepily if there was any rice left over from last night, Susan saying, No we ate it all, remember? and Melena groaning, But I'm hungry now, and Susan going, What do you want me to do, shit hot rice? We had to build a fire every day, which is easy: it has to be low and wide, not tall, so the grate fits over it good, and starting first with old paper bags or newspapers blown off the side of the road or moss if it wasn't too wet, then tiny twigs, then small twigs, then sticks, then big sticks, then a log once the big sticks were burning good. The sun would be up by the time the fire was made and we had its rays warming our backs and the fire warming our fronts, drinking tea and waiting for rice cream or miso soup or rice or millet, maybe brushing our hair if we remembered, but mostly no one remembered. There is a lot you can forget, living in a field.

We went to school more in the field, it was closer to town and Susan didn't mind so much about the gas money. Clambering over each other for the window seat or shotgun, singing to the radio. We caught rides off the highway easy, Andrew carrying the backpack of lunch, thermoses of rice, tortillas, rice cakes, trail mix but not the kind with chocolate chips unfortunately. No tofu sandwiches, because tofu needs refrigeration. If Susan had been in town to get supplies or do laundry she might pick us up, or we could take the school bus if we could convince the driver that the field was our bus stop, which made him look at us funny, like maybe we were runaways living in the forest and he should call the pigs on us, but he never did. After school we trekked back across the field to play games until dinnertime, in a cave made of bent-over willows, doing things we didn't want Helene or Susan to know about, like reading magazines we found or trying to smoke banana peels or dried mullein or just talking about food we wanted.

By dinnertime, which was whenever more of us were complaining than not complaining, we would be near the fire again, pulling on more sweaters if the sun was behind the trees. The crackling of the fire, porcelain spoons against pottery bowls or the wooden scrape of chopsticks. Beans with nettles or rice and sometimes a vegetable like carrots or squash cut into it, ground sesame seeds, toasted sunflower seeds, rice cakes. Wash the bowls with a little water sloshed into them from a jug, careful not to get grass or dirt into the bowls.

After eating, Helene would read stories from her book of Tibetan fables or tell koans, which are like riddles without answers. A prayer to the goddess and a prayer to the forest and poke the fire a little, Clanie, to remind it we're here. And finally we'd leave the warmth of the fire to crawl into our chilly sleeping bags, already a little damp, the smell of wood smoke in my clothes, a night breeze going through my hair, the whisper of a passing car, a small animal shuffling in the leaves, one of us sighing or sneezing. Maybe a cricket, and sleep.

In one place or another this was how we lived, never too close to town to be found out, never too far away because we needed to do laundry or get food stamps and food and maybe go to the library or dig through the free box. After a while we didn't go to school anymore, it seemed too far away, like another land.

Chapter 8

A Place of Lost and Broken Things

The place we live at longest is the abandoned ranch. I don't know how we end up there, we just do, up a narrow winding road that is first asphalt and then gravel and then dirt, hugging a mountain all the way up to its dry dusty top. Limp thistles and straggly black-eyed Susans and milkweed line the road, and madrones powdered gray with dust cling to the hillside. At the top of the mountain a shimmering sky hangs over a few shacks made of wood and tar paper and tin. Fields of dry brown grass stretch out around the ranch, circled far off by falling-down rusted barbed wire fences lined with crows and magpies.

The ranch property goes as far as I can see and is scattered with weird outer-space garbage. A dry hot place of broken things all eaten by sun and wind. Scraps of wood and rolls of tar paper laying on the ground with green-yellow grass and scurrying beetles underneath. Windows with the panes of glass missing and paint peeling off the wood, piles of plastic pipe, rotting barrels, half a gazebo gone gray and shiny, a falling-in sun deck, spare tires, a broken tractor. Parts of chairs, crates, an outdoor shower that trickles lukewarm water and has two sides missing. A ghost ranch. The wind whispers strangely and there's no one around.

We make our camp near the sun deck. We scavenge through the junk and find a car seat, and along with our crates, that is the living room. We drag a saggy warped table and some of the less broken chairs near that, plus a board across two flat rocks, and this is our dining room. Susan has a twelve-person army tent now and that's us kids' bedroom. We make a new fire circle and stash our kitchen stuff on the sun deck with the milk crates of rice and beans and sesame seeds and millet underneath, plus a sack of dried fruit and nuts that the moms decide has to go way way underneath so it's harder for us kids to get to. There are some carpet scraps, too, and a moth-eaten horse blanket, which we use like a carpet for the dirt. We sweep our dirt floor, too, sprinkling water on it first to keep from raising a cloud of dust. Near the sun deck a huge flowering rose geranium thrives in the hot sun and this makes our house beautiful and smell nice too. This smell goes all through the camp and this one piece of fragrant living beauty makes the camp a place I like, that and the dump.

Exploring the ranch, we find the place where people must have left all their worst junk and we climb through it like little rats, yelling and screeching. The dump has just about everything in it and we pick through it for days, hours in the sun falling away while we pore and peer, kicking over rotting boxes and bags and bending down to tug something or other, poking and prodding and wrinkling our noses and exclaiming. People think dumps are just full of garbage but they're way more than that. They're like

Kmart for poor people, a giant store where everything is free and you can take anything, and some of the things are fine for taking. Dumps aren't just trash. They're collections of things that used to be part of a life before. The thing you pick up and turn over in your hands and look at says something. At least to me. Half of a pair of fancy scissors, a curled-up shoe, the tassel from a lamp shade, a telephone ear piece, the guts of a radio, nail polish gone the color of cement, a cracked vase. A jar of peppers that must have sat in the sun for years, the peppers bleached white, smelling sharply of vinegar and something else, tainted and old. These things could have waited decades for someone to come along and pick them up and turn them over and shake them and open them up and then throw them away, hollering. Chipped bowls and old doorknobs. An umbrella bent inside out. Tired things dying very slowly because they were now useless. I rescue a lot of broken jars and put weeds and flowers in them, line up the doorknobs around our rose geranium, make a bent-metal forest out of old forks and spoons and saw blades and spatulas.

We spend the whole summer on the ranch and time becomes a different thing, spread out far and wide with no ending point, days melting into each other under the hot sun. The geranium bakes in the hot dry air while flies buzz around our heads and sweaty shoulder blades and land on old grains of rice and apple cores on the ground. For hours we sprawl out on the horse blanket and the car seat, feeling the sticky prickliness of the heat and listening to the drone of the flies and watching for a cloud in the glaring sky. I watch heat waves shimmer across the brown grass, only these indistinct phantoms breaking the expanse of sky and sun and time. The blackened ring of stones where we cook our food looks like something ancient, and so do the paths we wear randomly across the dry grass of the ranch.

There is an old water tower and I climb it even though I'm not supposed to and sit on the ledge up top beneath the conical roof, looking out across the fields for periods of time that might be years because there's no way to measure it, seeing across a distance that seems endless because there's no way to measure that, either. From the ledge as far as I can see there is the flat shimmer of infinite brown hills, and this plus the unmovingness of time gives me a certain feeling that I almost can't describe. The feeling is me in an empty place in an empty California, the low hills falling away into forever, waves of grass always moving over the hills in an eternal repeating pattern. The feeling is the sound of the high tuneless whistling of the wind moving through the grass without beginning or ending, me waiting for something that might never come, waiting for a pattern to the moving grass, listening for a song hidden beneath the tuneless whistle. Maybe it wasn't a feeling, just a hollow foreverness that had a shape around it, and the shape was me.

Only two things break the pattern of no pattern and those are the trips down the mountain for food and later a trip to the Rainbow gathering. Going into town we sing in the car, four six nine, the goose drank wine, the monkey chewed tobacco on the street car line, the line broke, the monkey got choked, and they all went to heaven in a little row boat. Let's sing "Amazing Grace" instead, Helene says, and pray for rice to fall out of the sky. We need rice to fall from the sky because you guys burn so much of it. I don't know how you do it, Clane, the rice is always raw on top, gummy in the middle, and burnt on the bottom. *Shut, up,* I think, *you're not my real mom. My real mom makes me cucumber and watercress tea sandwiches and lives in a house with a pool. And she lets me paint my toenails and wear white sandals with a little heel.*

Toward the end of the summer we travel down the mountain and along the coast highway to the Rainbow Gathering. Wheee, just us and thirty thousand of our closest friends, Helene says, tying up bundles of quilts and shoving pots and bowls in milk crates. We sing Bob Dylan songs and Grateful Dead songs and Beatles songs and stop for gas and then join a long line of cars pulling into a flat bare field full of hippies gathered around their cars unpacking things and saying, Hey sister, spare some doobage? Spare some change? The world could sure spare some change, Helene says, handing Ki over to me and telling us not to eat shitfood and saying, iI you get lost, just come back to the car or just look for us at a drum circle or find yourself someone nice to hang out with.

With Melena at my side holding Jude's hand and with Ki on my hip we wandered through crowds of people and teepees and tents and unlit fire circles and blankets spread out on the ground with stoned hippies laying everywhere or dancing or doing yoga or making out or hugging. There are booths offering massage and henna-ing and tie-dye and God's eyes and macrame and hand-thrown clay bowls and carved driftwood. There are tents that people stay, in and other tents used for gatherings of people holding hands and chanting, healers and aura sensings, chi readings, palm readings, ear piercings, face paintings, past-life readings. Places for hair braiding, tattooing, energy massage. Little kids run around naked with painted faces, people walk past in Renaissance costumes, dressed like Jesus, dressed like monks, dressed like fairies and damsels. A whole group of people wearing only burlap thongs, covered in mud and ash, chanting and tied together with rope, writhe and moan in fake but still scary agony and torture.

We wander for hours, watching reggae bands, drum circles, people making out, kids crying, dogs chasing Frisbees. Ki gets tired, I get hungry, and I find Helene somehow, sitting under a tree, stoned, with other stoned women, all of them with runes painted on them in red clay, waving feathers and chanting. I give Ki to Hlane and run off with Melena to find Matt and Haud to steal food. We steal as much as we can and pig out. Soy turkey and seitan and marinated tofu and pickles. The Hare Krishna food is the best. It's free, we don't have to steal it. You sit in a circle waiting and the Krishnas carry around five-gallon plastic buckets of curry and lentils and stewed fruit. We ear like little wolves and then lay under trees holding our stomachs and groaning. When it gets dark we find the moms where they made beds for us. We put on sweaters and then walk around to the different fire circles and dancing circles and storytelling circles. People sing Om Shiva Namaya and Michael Row the Boat Ashore and Kumbaya, and late in the night I fall asleep to that, the sound of different people singing all over the place, the glow of fires all the way across the fields.

Everyone sleeps late and I wake up feeling bloated and achy and dizzy. I have a hard time standing up. My legs are all trembly, I say to Helene. I think I'm sick. You're not sick, she says, You kids never get sick because you eat so much good clean dirt you're immune to germs. I follow Helene to different booths and whine for water and look for a place to lie in the shade, and sounds come from a long way off and light seems to be bouncing off everything right into my eyes, giving me a headache and making me sick to my stomach. Helene is arguing with a woman offering scrimshaw, going, That's negative death energy, using whale bone, that's dead whale. You're the negative energy here, the lady tells Helene, Send it back, send it back, I'm sending the negative energy back to you. I follow a cloud of white light squiggles back to our beds and fall asleep in a pile of covers hot from the sun and sleep unevenly and sweatily all day, not even interested in tofu ice cream and vegetable burgers. When it's time to go I drag myself to the car and Helene says, You really are sick. You're sick because you pigged out. That's what happens when you pig out. Us kids being all squished in the backseat makes me feel worse, and on the drive up to the mountain I ask Susan to stop the car and I got out to throw up and then crouch behind the car, drool coming out of my mouth, dust settling in the air around me. I doze and sweat all the way up the mountain and wake up only when the car doors are slamming shut. No fair, Clane has to carry stuff too, Haud says, and Matt says, She's faking it, and Andrew says, She's sulking, and Helene says, Well let her sulk. *Shut up*, I said to myself, *you're not my real mom. My real mom would tuck me into a white lace bed in a gazebo that isn't falling apart and give me green grapes and put a cold cloth on my head.* I fall asleep in another pile of quilts and sleep all evening and all night and wake up first in the morning, feeling fine, and go rummaging for green grapes but of course there aren't any, but there are green apples and I steal two.

Chapter 9

Never Straight, Only Forward

One day toward the end of this long summer on the abandoned ranch us kids are squatting underneath a pine tree looking for the place where we think Susan buried the big care package of candy and cookies that Susan's straight mom sent to the kids. Me and Andrew are taking turns digging with a broken army shovel while Melena holds Jude's hand, standing at the edge of the hole and keeping him from falling in. We knew better than to protest when Susan and Helene looked through the box and said, We're gonna have to bury this to keep the kids from flipping out on sugar. The last thing we need is you kids on sugar trips.

We kids just looked at each other and kept straight faces because it's better to just go along with the moms. Arguing leads to longer lectures and then having to give in anyway. We even tried to look like we all agreed, nodding our heads wisely, Yeah, white sugar and white flour is no good for us. All but Haud, who had been the first into the box even though it wasn't his, ripping into it like a crazed loony. Haud bounced up and down on his toes in mindless frustration when Susan took the box and then stalked off, and he was the first to decide that we were going to dig for the box, triumphantly holding the shovel up and saying, I know where it is. I found this at the dump and we're gonna dig for it. The box. I know where they buried the box.

He and Matt are scurrying around in the dry pine needles and brush underneath the trees looking for clues. When they don't find any, they just kind of make them up to keep our search interesting, because it's kind of a desperate search with no real hope of finding the box but we all really need something to do. We're starting to freak out.

The boys have been trying to build an airplane or spaceship to fly us out of here, gathering likely-looking scraps of tin and wood and a windshield that's only partly cracked. This will be the gear box, Haud says, staggering up with a huge chunk of ancient tractor engine which I can't identify. And this'll be the intake manifold, Matt says, pointing to a muffler that's full of holes. Andrew at first disagrees saying, You can't make a spaceship that works, stupid, that won't work. But there's really nothing else to do so we all go along and help gather parts that Haud keeps saying we'll need. We gotta have a rotor for the jet engine, he says, wrestling part of a piston out of a milk crate of filthy rusty loose parts. Gotta have a solid chassis. Haud's such a maniac, he's so sure we can build this, that we have to go along, first just playing and then somehow thinking that we can actually do it, dividing up into teams for reconnaissance and scouring the ranch for parts. That's how Haud found the place he thinks the box is buried.

So we're covered in dirt and we're cursing and sweating and starting to give in to the knowledge that we really aren't going to find the box when we hear a truck coming up the hill. A big truck is toiling up the hill, slow and heavy, you can tell by the sound of it changing into a lower gear. We run out into the road to watch it coming, it has to be coming here because the road just kind of ends here. There's never traffic on this road. There's a huge dust cloud rising above the pine and oak trees, and the truck is changing gears again and the sound of the engine is evening out as the road gets flatter. It's a big red truck with a bearded mustached man sitting high in the cab and bouncing along with the ruts. The truck grinds to stop and the engine is turned off and it starts to creak and the man gets out. Something about him looks really familiar as he's climbing out of the truck and then I realize it's Claude, it's our dad. He always drives big trucks. Here he is all of a sudden, just like Helene does too, comes from out of nowhere with a silly grin on his face. Do everyone's parents come like that?

Claude looks scruffy with his long beard and mustache and a bent cowboy hat over long hair and that's pretty much how he always looks. Right then I know things are going to get different. Things always get different when one of our parents comes or leaves and we switch between them. We haven't switched for a long time and up here on the ranch I guess I've forgotten about him. I haven't seen him since I was seven or eight, since before Ki was born. Maybe I saw him when I was nine but I can't remember for sure.

Haud starts capering around the truck like a little horse, pawing at the dirt with his feet and rearing his head up and down in the air. Claude looks at us with his hands in his pockets and then he takes some tobacco out of his shirt, Bugler, and starts rolling a cigarette. Feeling shy, I awkwardly hug Claude around his legs. He lights his cigarette and starts to puff on it, spits out a piece of tobacco. He pats the truck and starts showing it to us, saying, Got this baby for a song and it's going to get us all the way back to New Mexico. Am I going? Haud asks, jumping up and down on the running board and hanging on the door handle. This is an International Harvester three-quarter-ton flatbed dump truck, Claude says, and switches the truck back on and shows us kids how the flatbed lifts up in the air and then turns it off again. I flew out here to California to buy it, he says, lifting up the hood. The boys all climb up to look at the engine while Claude fiddles with things and Melena and I hang around watching. Where's your mom, he says, finally closing the hood and looking at us. I'm Claude, who are you, he says to Melena, and he tries to take Jude's hand but Jude is shy and starts to drool and he backs away shaking his head.

Claude stays with us just overnight. He walks around our place looking at things, always smoking a cigarette, kicking at things, stumps, rocks, finally looking out over the fields for a while. We follow him, me and Haud, everywhere he goes, Haud hanging off his arm, hanging on his leg, stepping on his shoes going walk me walk me walk me. I explain things to him, saying, Here's our dump, here's the space ship we're building, here's the shitter, which is just a big trench in the ground with a board over it. What are you doing here,? we ask, How long are you staying,? Did you come from New Mexico? When are you going back? Can we go with you?

Helene doesn't seem surprised to see Claude. She looks up from some embroidery she's working on in the falling-in gazebo and says, Greetings. The prodigal father returns. Claude squats on the floor next to her and fingers the embroidery and smokes and they talk. They argue about money and argue about the food we eat and argue about whether we kids are staying with her or going with him. They both yell at us to go away and then they argue some more, we can see their mouths moving and Helene's arms waving in the air and Claude chain-smoking. I can't help but wonder how he found us but all I really care about is if we get to go with him, do we get to eat anything we want?

He sits by the fire with us when we cook dinner, millet and toasted sunflower seeds and sheets of green-black wakame toasted over the fire, which we wrap around the millet and eat like burritos and which I hate because wakame tastes fishy. I hate seaweed. Claude is mostly quiet and Helene is mostly quiet and Susan doesn't say much and neither do any of the kids except Haud. Haud keeps talking about the spaceship, telling Claude how the intake manifold has two thousand horsepower, no twenty thousand horsepower, no a million horsepower, and how the suspension is double rack and pinion, and how the navigation is inertial and gyroscopic and has radar too.

Claude keeps nodding at Haud's crazy spaceship talk and trying to shovel millet in his mouth with his chopsticks, but millet is really hard to eat with chopsticks and he drops a lot in his lap. Jude is watching Claude with his mouth open, drooling millet and spit and bits of seaweed, and then he wobbles to his feet and moves around the fire to get to the millet in Claude's lap but he trips over Claude's legs and falls. He falls close to the fire and his arm goes across the hot rocks and he tries to howl in pain but only a soundless moaning grunt comes out and everyone is moving, Claude trying to pull Jude up and Susan springing to her feet and reaching across the fire to get Jude away from it, singeing her long hair in the flames. Jude is blubbering drooly snotty tears and Helene is screeching about Claude's negative energy, how Claude's bad vibes are causing a psychic disturbance that upsets Jude. Jude's arm is burnt pretty bad and Claude's face is pulled tight and dark and scowly, the firelight reflecting off his glasses and turning his face into a devil face with burning flames for eyeholes. Melena is crying, Susan rocks Jude in her lap, and there's no ice to put on his burn but Helene rubs salve across it all the while talking about how this isn't Jude's karma, it's Claude's karma. Everyone goes to bed quiet, just the sound of kids snuffling tears. Claude sleeps in the truck.

In the morning Claude leaves. He takes Haud with him. I don't know for sure how this got decided but I hear parts of Claude and Helene's argument about it. Helene says how Haud is going out of his tree up here on the ranch, how his yang energy is more compatible with Claude's yang, how Haud just isn't into our trip here and how Claude isn't either. Why don't they go off to New Mexico and eat a lot of meat and sugar and build earth-destroying trucks together. How Haud had earlier found a bottle of plum wine Susan had been saving and had drunk the whole thing and passed out and then got really sick, which I didn't know about at all. Haud's out of his gourd.

Haud's stuff, a sleeping bag and some clothes, get wrapped up in a burlap sack and thrown in the back of the cab, behind the seat. Claude and Haud get into the truck, Haud's butt crack showing above his too-loose pants. He stands up on the seat all excited, jumping up and down until he bonks his head on the roof of the cab and Claude says, For chrissakes settle down already.

All the kids gather at the side of the road to wave at them as they leave. My chest goes all tight and achy and I feel a huge hole open up inside me. It seems like an old and familiar feeling, something I know from when I was little, like when I was living with Claude in New Mexico and he would go somewhere and be gone for a long time and I would look for him all over the place and then sit by the side of the road waiting for him to come back or walking around the valley all day asking people, Have you seen my dad?

After they go I sit by the side of the road for a long time, thinking I hear the truck coming back up the hill, that the truck will come grinding up the hill and Claude will pop his head out of the window and say, Hey Clanie we almost forgot you. Climb on in. Sitting there in the dirt, I fall into myself, into the hole in my chest. They're gone without me and I'm nothing but a giant hole. I stay a hole for a long time. I think all the time about Claude and Haud driving down the highway, and in my mind I see the headlights of oncoming cars turning Claude's glasses into shiny silver holes, driving forever. Helene says, Stop moping. You're just thinking about all that shitfood Claude feeds you.

Jude's arm heals but he's acting weird. All of us are acting weird. Matt keeps peeing in his sleeping bag, Melena is as skinny as a stick, I sit for hours living inside my own head, making up a different life. Jude keeps getting up in the middle of the night, crying and peeing on himself, trying to crawl into different people's sleeping bags. He stops eating, thin as a little bird with no feathers. Susan tries to tempt him with sweet tea and toast but he won't eat and just cries. Helene is typical about it, going on about karma from a past life or kidney problems manifesting as depression. They decide to take Jude to a guru to cleanse him of Claude's negative energy, some macrobiotic monk guy who would be able to say why Jude was flipping out like this. Helene and Susan argue about taking him to the hospital. No way should you take him to the hospital, Helene says, Western medicine is death culture.

We all pile into Susan's car to take Jude down the mountain and inland to the monk or sage or guru, whatever he is, in Sonoma. I want to go because if we go to town there's always the chance we'll go to the store and if we go to the store there's always the chance of goodies, maybe rice cake and yinnie syrup sandwiches or tamari corn chips or plum candy. Did I say what yinnie syrup is? It's brown rice syrup, just like honey only not made by bees and so not an animal product. I'm not crazy about yinnie syrup but it's better than nothing. It's called yinnie syrup because it's yin.

It's hot on top of the mountain but it gets hotter as we go down into the valley, the height of summer, a sun with no end and dust on everything. The car windows are down for the air but the dust fills the car and our clothes are covered. I notice all of a sudden that all of our clothes are worn out and holey and tattered. Even my green bell bottoms that were almost new when I was in Monte Rio are shredded now, a hole in the knee and one in the butt. Melena and I amuse ourselves by talking about clothes we want while Andrew reads and Matt sings to himself. Haud always sings the wrong words on purpose and yells too loud but now I wish he was here to do that, singing isn't the same without him.

It gets even hotter as we drive inland away from the coast. Jude's sweaty hair is plastered to his forehead and he sleeps restlessly on Helene's lap. We have to go straight here, Susan says, and Helene says, Never straight, only forward. The first time I knew that word, *straight*, I didn't know it could mean directions, I thought it only meant straight people living straight lives. I can't even remember what a straight life is like now. Oak trees whiz by, poplars, then vineyards full of grapes hanging heavily in perfectly even rows. Vineyards are great to watch from a car. It looks like you're at the wide end of a fan, traveling along the edge of the fan, and the rows of vines make up the spines of the fan, all leading to a narrow central point. That's called perspective, Andrew says, looking up from his book.

We get to a compound kind of place where the guru is, a few trailer-like buildings scattered around a kind of courtyard in the center. A tired-looking person in monk robes and a straw hat is raking a thin patch of gravel around a big rock, all of it a little bare and sorry-looking. If this guru guy is so great how come he doesn't have a marble palace like in my book of Indian myths, like the Taj Mahal, or a banyan tree like Siddhartha's? He's forsaken all worldly goods, Helene says impatiently, getting out of the car and setting Jude down on his thin legs. Now you kids don't fuss and disturb the monks.

We sit on some bamboo mats for a long time in the sun. I try not to shift and fidget because I want the monks to see what an enlightened person I am, sitting in the lotus position with my hands cupped saying om quietly. I breathe deep like Helene says and try to do meditation but it's hard because I'm thinking about all of the fat green grapes around us, grapes and lemonade and melon and strawberry milkshakes. Tuna fish sandwiches. Helene always says my cravings for shitfood show how sanpaku I am. Sanpaku means sick, sick in the soul, permanently sick. You are sanpaku if the bottoms of your corneas don't touch the lower rim of your eyelids. Mine don't touch. You're sanpaku if the white of the eye can be seen between the cornea and the rim.

When we finally go in to see the guru I make sure to only look up at him, keeping my head tilted way back, so he won't see my sanpaku eyes. I expect to see some blinding aura around him because he's enlightened, but he's only a skinny brown guy wearing tai chi pants and a white tee shirt. Sitting cross-legged, he looks carefully at Jude, holding Jude's head in his hands, looking at Jude's eyes, his lips, and then his fingernails. Give the boy potatoes, the guru says. Give him only potatoes. His hands are bent and gnarled and his head is bald and tanned. Give the boy only potatoes.

We buy potatoes on the way back, but just potatoes, no treats. Normally we're not allowed potatoes because they're too yin. Yin is the feminine principle, the contracted and the yielding and the passive. All root vegetables are yin because they develop underground, like potatoes and carrots and beets. Can we have potatoes too, all the kids ask Helene when Jude gets boiled potatoes for dinner. No, you kids get rice. Rice is all you need, have a rice day, she says.

We boil potatoes for Jude, we bake potatoes for Jude, wrapping them in foil and putting them in the coals of our cooking fire, we put them in miso broth for him, we fry them in safflower oil. Jude won't eat. He goes back to the guru and this time the guru says give him anything he wants but he still doesn't eat.

This leads to a showdown between Helene and Susan and is how we move away from the mountain and away from Susan and Jude and Matt and Melena and Andrew and how we never see them again. Susan wants to take Jude to a regular doctor and Helene doesn't want her to. Susan accuses Helene of being dogmatic and Helene accuses Susan of being uptight. Yeah well it's my uptight food stamps we're living on and my uptight car we drive in, says Susan. Sister, you need to work this negative energy out, Helene keeps saying. You're the one carrying the negative energy here, Susan says. I can't keep living up here on this godforsaken pile of dirt, Susan says, the kids need school and interaction and socialization. You mean they need Social Security numbers, Helene says. You mean they need government support. Well, government support is what's keeping you fed, Susan says. Everything gets packed up and we drive down the mountain for the last time, and Susan drops us off at the post office in Guerneville and drives off without saying anything, Melena looking out the back window of the car at us with her face white and scared. I never see them again.

Chapter 10
Love Is Like Oxygen

Don't ask me how or why, but where we end up for the rest of the summer and almost into fall is Cotati. Cotati is near Santa Rosa in Sonoma County, a small flat town with a lot of parking lots and drab low buildings and big stores like Kmart and Sears. In the center of town is a grassy shady park but then the rest of the town seems like one big mall baking under the sun, a big mall and a lot of aluminum warehouses and housing tracts without trees. Acres of pavement and straight flat highways.

There's a trailer park near the University of Sonoma at the edge of town and that's where we go. The same trailer park, in fact, that we lived in when Bruce and Helene were still together and they had just turned macrobiotic. Sonoma Grove Trailer Park looks the same, not bad, even kind of nice. It's surrounded by poplars that line a dirt road all the way around the park, and along the poplars is a tall redwood fence that hides the highway. It's neat and even and clean, and after the ranch I like neat and clean and even. There's a little road that makes a figure eight through the park, and grass and a little tree on all the plots, and two redwood bathhouses, one at each end, and a big community building. The community building has a stone floor and tremendous big windows with window seats and a fireplace so huge you can climb into it, and clunky leather couches and long tables for people to eat together and a kitchen anyone can use.

The trailer park hadn't seemed so nice when we lived there before. We stayed in a trailer then, a sorry little green thing that seemed to crouch on the ground like a puppy with a sore butt, hunched up and trying to hide. It had horizontal slats that didn't open up for windows and ratty green carpet, curtains in a pattern that looked like moldy pot holders, and awful imitation wood paneling.

This time we stay in a tent, a little orange one that I guess we got from Susan. Our stuff is all still rolled up and in bags, and I'm digging around in the bags looking for a hairbrush, untying the bedroll, spilling books and embroidery all over. The light in the tent is all orangey and hot and airless and musty with the smell of molding books and smoke from our campfires. I really need to find the hairbrush because it occurs to me that now that we're not on the abandoned ranch in the middle of nowhere we should try to look less grimy and dusty and ratty. I need to brush my hair before going to the bathhouse to wash, and I need to brush Ki's hair, too, and we need to bathe before we can go looking in the free box for some newer clothes. It's bad enough digging for people's leftovers in the free box, no way am I going to let us look like animals while we do it. I'm thinking I saw a teddy bear for Ki.

I give up in disgust and take Ki to the spigot on our plot and I'm using water to smooth my hair down, knuckling the water out of my eyes, and someone says, Do you always brush your hair with water? I look up and there's a girl there, my age, a pretty girl with dark freckly skin and a fantastic mop of curly black hair and slanty lazy-looking eyes. She's chewing gum slowly, making it pop, and leaning against the little guardrail that goes around the tarmac road, leaning on it as if she has better things to do than stand up straight and anyhow doesn't care, isn't nervous like I definitely would be, talking to a new person.

No, I say, I can't find my hairbrush. We just moved and all our stuff is still packed. She says my name's Nickie and I'm twelve and you can come to my house and use mine if you want. How old are you? Twelve, I think, I say, peering at her from under my rat's nest of soggy hair. She has a turny-uppy nose. Turny-uppy noses are the best. Nickie. Her name is soooo cool. Then I have to go take off after Ki right away because she's scurrying straight toward a big bucket of what looks like tar in the next plot. I don't get to her in time and Ki has her hands plunged all the way into the bucket of warm tar, spreading it on her cheeks and legs. Oh no, I wail, Helene's gonna kill me. Who's Helene? Nickie asks, following me and hunkering down near Ki to inspect the mess. Helene's my mom. Why do you call her Helene and not Mom? I call my mom Mom, she says, snapping her gum, but just conversationally, not mean. We look at Ki and Ki looks up at us, smiling, and Nickie says, Let's take her to my mom's boyfriend. He paints and he has turpentine and turpentine will get that off.

I lead Ki and follow Nickie. Her mom's boyfriend is sitting in a deck chair dabbing paint onto a board propped on a chair in front of him, he's smearing colors together into a rainbow, and the ground around him is covered in rainbow paintings on all kinds of pieces of wood. He barely notices us, just tokes on a doobie, getting a little paint on his lip, nodding at us when we take the turpentine can. We spend a long time getting the tar off Ki, and after a while she is crying and trying to get away but no way can I let Helene see her like this. She is always getting into gooey stuff, she loves it, she'll sit in a mud puddle for hours. All the while Nickie talks. I'm going to shave my legs like my mom, she says, are you? Do you have hair down there? Where did you come from? Do you have more sisters and brothers? Luckily she says more about herself than she asks me. She says she is half black, her father's black and her mom is white, and she has a sister named Sierra like the mountains. She shows me her place which is a little pink-and-white trailer around the corner.

Nickie's mom is never around and Helene is never around —she's hanging out with some dude—so we spend a lot of time together, taking care of Ki and Sierra. We bring coloring books and pencils and markers to the big table in the community building, we raid the free box every day, we steal change from our moms' purses to buy junk at the 7-11 down the highway. Like some kind of bug coming out of the walls, wherever Nickie goes boys appear, because she's so pretty with her cute nose and floppy mop of hair and slanty eyes. I'm not jealous. Mostly it's Paul and

Derrick, who are brothers and live in a school bus in the park. We horse around on the couches and Paul says he knows where there's a TV we can watch in a little room off the rec room at the side of the building. You need a key, Nickie accuses. No, sometimes it's open, Derrick says, sprawled on the couch. We find the room and watch *Electric Company* and *Romper Room*. I looooove TV, which I've never really seen before, but Helene flips out when she catches me singing A is for apple J is for jacks, cinnamon toasted apple jacks.

The trips to 7-11 with stolen change are the best, the most fun, in a scared guilty kind of way. Whenever we gather anything close to a dollar we take off to spend it, never taking bills because they might be missed, but our moms don't seem to miss nickels and quarters and dimes here and there, and we find a lot of change in the couch of the community building too. We walk down the gravel on the side of the highway with big trucks whizzing by, the eighteen wheelers and pickup trucks tossing little rocks up at us and blasting us with hot air.

Inside the store I'm always dazzled by the brightness and the amount of all the things on the shelves. The outside world is normal colors but inside the store it's a waterfall, a flood, a storm of color, the candy bars and bags of chips and boxes of cookies and packets of this and cans of that. I always have a hard time choosing and no matter what I get I wish I'd gotten something else. Strawberry Slurpees, Snickers, Three Musketeers, Charleston Chews, Butterfingers, Oreos, Twinkies, Ho Ho's,

Zingers, Lay's barbecue potato chips, Ruffles potato chips, Fritos corn chips. We eat sitting on the sidewalk beside the store so no one catches us in the trailer park. Sometimes we take our loot back to the park, hidden in our shirts, and we go to Paul and Derrick's bus because if we give them some they let us watch the *The Muppet Show* with them. *The Muppet Show* is the greatest thing I've ever seen. Wearing too-small corduroy cutoffs, swinging my legs against the bunk bed in the bus, warm with the sun, my mouth stuffed full of shortbread cookies and chocolate milk, I'm happy and, I look for the word, normal. Derrick says, Hey chicken legs, and puts his fat paw on my thigh, all brown from the sun, and says, I like your legs. I look down at myself and think, Those are my legs, I'm a girl and I have a body and this is my body.

Nickie tells me it's time for us to shave our legs and tells me we should shave under our arms too and says, That's what girls have to do. I saw it on TV. The next time I see her she's stolen her mom's razor and she tried to shave but got it wrong somehow and there's great bloody strips torn off her legs and she's crying. We're sitting on the guardrail in front of our tent and I'm patting her arm while she's crying and Helene comes in and says, What happened to you, girlie? Nickie tells her and Helene says, Once you shave you have to keep shaving, it's better not to, and puts comfrey salve on Nickie's legs. Nickie goes home still snuffling and Helene goes over to Tom's place.

Tom lives near us in a little wooden gypsy house built onto the back of a pickup truck. This is where Helene spends most of her time, with Tom Starchild. He's very tall and very thin and very quiet and always has a little sleepy half-smile on his face. He's maybe as old as Helene, with salt-and-pepper hair like hers, long and hanging in his face and strung with beads and feathers like hers, and he wears amulets and robes like she does too, except when he wears jeans with a huge belt buckle with a lion's head on it for Leo, because he's a Leo, and then he's bare-chested and his skinny ribs stick out from his gaunt chest. He's worse macrobiotic then Helene, only eating rice and sunflower seeds and Braggs Liquid Aminos. He has tons of bracelets that jingle on his arms, and rings with more lions' heads on them, and big bunches of keys hanging from his belt.

Tom has a little propane stove in his gypsy car,t and Helene mostly moves in with him and me and Ki mostly stay in the tent. Helene plants morning glory seeds at the side of his cart and they grow big and wild up over the roof, and Tom says he's going to harvest and dry the seeds and make them into tea that gets you really really high. What gets you the highest? I want to know, and he says, A man and a woman making love gets you highest.

Because Helene is preoccupied with Tom she doesn't notice me as much and I steal a lot of change and spend a lot of time with Nickie at her place, depending on her for leftovers of barbecue and Chinese food because Tom's macrobiotic isn't enough food to live on. We listen to the radio in the community building, Love is like oxygen, you get too much you get too high, not enough and you're gonna die, wearing our tube tops from the free box. Helene catches me wearing the tube top and says, No way you're wearing that, it's rayon and it's too flashy. Instead of putting it back in the free box I stuff it way down in my bag of clothes.

We convince Helene to let us go to a roller-skating rink near Cotati. Fine, she says, but no eating shitfood from the snack bar, and by the way, how are you getting there? Nickie knows the bus, I say, and Helene goes back to what she's doing, which is burning her menstrual rags. Why are you doing that, I ask, confused, because she's cursing and swearing and squinting her eyes against the smoke. Tom says it's sacred, she says, and I shrug and run off to find Nickie.

We wait all afternoon on the highway for the Number 49 Sonoma County Transit bus, and when it comes huffing to a stop we fling ourselves into seats and sit grinning and sweating. I know how to roller-skate good because I did it all the time in San Francisco when I was young.

Inside the rink, which is a big tin hut that has a rounded top, like a can on its side, it's dark and there's music playing loud, Rockin' chair, let me be your rockin' chair. Colored lights flash from the DJ booth and a mirror ball revolves from the ceiling, throwing squares across the skaters as they go around the rink. It's big. It's fun. It's great. My heart is pounding as we rent skates and change into them and glide, a little clumsy at first, onto the rink and pause at the fence to look at everyone going by, and then, the same way we flung ourselves onto the bus, we fling ourselves, whooping, into the thick of the skaters on the rink, arms flailing, hair flying.

There are crowds of kids. There's a big knot of black girls, all wearing satin jackets that say Brown Sugar and Hot Chocolate and Cinnamon Girl, all skating backwards together, swaying in time to the music, which is now going Fly robin fly, and then there's screaming as That's the way, uh-huh uh-huh, I like it, comes on. There are tall pretty girls with long legs wearing tight Dittos and tube tops, tossing their heads of long curly hair, checking over their shoulders for who's watching them, and there are fast clumps of boys who dart around each other, skating like mad, arms and legs pumping and swinging out to the side, and there are boys hanging on the fence flipping through their hair with big combs and grinning at each other like idiots. Couples skate gets called by the DJ and I'm frantic to find someone I want to skate with but I don't know anyone and no way am I going to do what Nickie is doing, which is standing saucily in front of a crowd of boys at the fence, arms crossed over her chest to make her tiny boobs look bigger, calling, Hey you, in the purple shirt, wanna skate? He skates with her, grinning stupidly, and I watch people line up at the snack bar, smelling nachos, pickles, hot dogs, my mouth watering.

We skate until we have blisters on our heels and our mouths are parched dry and our lips are chapped and the sun is going down. We're too tired on the bus to even talk, though Nickie grins at me sleepily and I grin back at her just as tiredly and we ride with our heads against the glass, watching the lights of the Kmart come on, the lights of the Sears come on, the lights of the Auto Mart come on, the lights at the drive-in hamburger stand. Hamburgers, I'm thinking, the kind with the dry little patty and the limp little pickle slices and pale floppy lettuce and too-sweet buns, all squished flat and greasy in a paper bag, mmmmm. Helene gives me rice and toasted sunflower seeds wrapped in corn tortillas at Tom's truck when I come in, and Ki comes to sit in my lap and show me her mud pies. She points to them, pretend baking, on the running board of the truck. Fat Stephen goes walking by, wearing only a towel and flip-flops, on his way to the showers. I bet he has a hairy butt.

Chapter 11

Spaces Between Places

Nickie's all bummed out one day, but kind of excited, too. We're moving to Oregon, she announces, flopping down on the grass at the door of the orange tent, where I'm trying to brush burrs out of Ki's hair from when we went exploring in the field behind the trailer park. All we found were abandoned trailers, but the field was full of wild sunflowers baking in the heat and it smelled good, the dusty pollen dancing around in the air and the tough leaves scratching our arms but shading us, too. Nickie's mom says they're moving to Oregon to get ready for tree-planting season and so her mom's boyfriend can sell art to the tourists at a big flea market.

Nickie and I decide we have to have a party and we have a great plan about how to do it: all afternoon we knock on trailer doors, holding an empty coffee can and saying we're collecting donations for a children's party. It's not really lying, exactly, is how my reasoning goes, because we are children and we are going to have a party. We get something like eight dollars and fly down the road to the 7-11 and buy just about everything in the store, two big sacks of chips and candy and cookies and soda. We drag camp chairs and sleeping bags and a transistor radio to the grass outside of Nickie's trailer. As the sun is just starting to sink we run around to Paul and Derrick's bus and bang on the side and tell them we're having a slumber party. Flopped on the grass, we listen to the radio, Barry Manilow and the Bee Gees and Carol King, and stuff ourselves with food and chug sodas. This is way different from the ranch, I'm thinking. This is so much better. Heeeere at the Copa, Copa Cabana. Nickie sits on Derrick's lap and kisses him, spilling Fritos, and then she jumps up shrieking, Okay, now you have to kiss Clane. He sits down and shoves a Snickers bar into his mouth and says I can't now, I'm eating. You kiss her, Paul. Paul is fiddling with the radio and then it's Love is like oxygen. I didn't want to kiss Paul, anyway, he's fat, and I like Scott Baio way better. Everyone talks about how to hump. As it gets darker I lay in my sleeping bag, watching for falling stars and feeling guilty because Ki might miss me, while Paul snorts next to me and Nickie and Derrick squirm around in two sleeping bags zipped together, whispering and rustling.

We're woken up by the sun shining in our faces, puffy from sleep, the taste of Lay's barbecue potato chips still on my tongue. In the bathhouse Nickie pulls me into a shower stall and we crouch on the damp cement floor while Nickie whispers that she and Derrick did it last night. I'm not a virgin anymore, she says, I'm a woman now. Liar, I accuse her, but I'm not so sure. Gross, I think, images of fat Steven's hairy butt and Derrick's big thing going around in my head. What did it feel like? I ask. Good, she breathes, eyes all crazy. Derrick said I'm a good lay. He said I'm a good fuck.

All of a sudden Nickie's gone, just like that. I wasn't even there when she left, I was probably digging in the free box or looking for leftover food in the community kitchen. Now going to 7-11 by myself seems more like sneaking than playing, and watching the TV in the rec room is weird and lonely by myself. Derrick and Paul are gone somewhere, maybe to their dad's.

I find a way to climb up on top of the bathhouse and I sit up there on the roof at dusk, watching the traffic crawl by slowly on the distant highway. Far off I can see the buildings of Sonoma State University, lit up at night and looking like the alien landing strip in *Close Encounters of the Third Kind*. The sound of the traffic is almost like crying, trucks crying to themselves, crying down the highway. This makes me feel like California is this huge state at the end of the world, like there are a million spaces between the places the trucks are going, California is all space at the edge of nothing.

Over at the southern edge of the trailer park where I haven't gone before I meet Lisa and Chardonay, two more girls with cute, normal names, girls I never met before. I wish I had a normal name and I try out Jackie to myself, and Elaine, and Amber.

I meet Lisa and Chardonay for the first time in the community kitchen. Chardonay is using the blender to make what looks like a strawberry smoothie, and it makes my mouth water so much I have to ask what it is. Strawberry daiquiri, she says, spooning some into her mouth. It's hooch, she says, want some? She dips the spoon back into the blender and hands it to me, spilling some on the floor, which she wipes up by running her sandal across it until it's smeared into a pale blur on the floor. It's bitter and I spit it out in surprise. My boyfriend gets me the booze, she says, pouring the daiquiri into a Slurpee cup and licking the side of the blender. I'm Chardonay and that's Lisa, my sister. She points to Lisa, who's sitting on the counter, swinging her legs and stuffing a candy bar almost whole into her mouth. Chardonay looks like one of the roller-rink girls, long blond hair, tight Dittos bell bottoms and a tee shirt that says If it ain't Stiff it ain't worth a fuck, on the front, and Stiff Records on the back. Lisa is skinny and flat like me, with her hair cut like Dorothy Hamill. She's swinging her hair against her cheeks while she chews, her cheeks bulging, watching me, and then she pops the last bite into her mouth and wipes her face and says, Chardonay is Mounds because she's got the tits and I'm Almond Joy 'cause even though I'm flat I'm sweet as candy. Chardonay does have big old boobs under that shirt.

They both live in a school bus. Their mom smokes Pall Malls all day and wears her sunglasses inside the bus and is always saying damnitalltohell where's that child-support check and here girls, Kool-Aid. I'm into the Kool-Aid and also into the baloney sandwiches she gives us. For days the sky stays the same bright cloudless blue and we swing in a hammock strung between two skinny plum trees that bend visibly with our weight, drinking Kool-Aid while the girls talk about boys.

I go into town with Chardonay and her boyfriend Hitch and Lisa, in Hitch's car, which has a bumper sticker that says, If My Ride Is Rockin' Don't Come Knockin'. Hitch is named Harry for real and is always giving Chardonay hickeys, even while he drives, Chardonay leaning into him on the front seat, an arm flung across his shoulders, while Lisa and I nudge each other in the backseat and pick at bits of stuffing that's coming out of the car seats. The Kmart parking lot is miles wide and roasting hot under the sun, and inside it's too cold from all the air conditioning. Goose bumps jump right out on my skin. We try on flowery bikinis and Lisa shows me how she has hair down there around her veejay, and Chardonay stuffs lacy bras down Lisa's bra and says, You're walking out of here like you own the place, understand? In the jewelry aisles I slip bracelets and necklaces off the little stands and slip them superfast into my pants. Thin bright music echoes faintly in the aisles and there are skinny women in pantsuits watching us closely. After a while one comes up to ask may I help you? and Lisa and Chardonay give her withering smiles and say, No thank you, we're just looking. I've become expert at stealing from the 7-11 but this time I know we're going to get caught. It's too late to do anything but walk out like we own the place, which we do, and then we're busted. The heat hits us like a solid white wave of energy, so bright that at first I can't see the man who puts his hand on my shoulder and says, Excuse me Miss, would you step back into the store please. Ladies, just come right into this office if you don't mind. The three of us wail and sob, but I'm the only one doing it for real. I tuck my freezing cold skinny shoulders into my purple tie-dye tee shirt and make a tent out of it with my knees and stick my head into the tent and heave huge sobs. The store detective who busted us is calling the cops on us. He's also trying to call our moms, but there's nothing but pay phones at the trailer park. Bright fluorescent light from overhead is bouncing off the bald spot in the detective's hair. He looks at the three of us girls crying, Chardonay with eyeliner dripping down her face, and then he gestures to the cop who's just come in, a thin pimply guy who looks like he's going to fall over from the weight of all the stuff on his belt. We're going for a ride down to the station, girls, the cop says, thumbs hooked in his belt. We all start crying again. We're going to jail, Lisa shrieks, and we scurry out to the cop car, parked in front with its roof lights revolving slowly and a crowd of curious shoppers in front of it.

But the cop just drives us back to the trailer park and drops us off with our moms. Thank you officer, Helene says brightly, taking me by the hand. She just happens to be around for once, not smoking joints in the cart with Tom or burning menstrual rags or meditating naked. Farfuckinout, Clanie, she says, shaking my hand up in the air over my head. You're growing up, getting busted by the pigs for liberating corporate property for the people. For the first time I'm thinking she's kind of a cool mom after all.

This feeling lasts as long as it takes for her to catch me eating a Chocodile I've liberated from the 7-11. She catches me stuffing the last bite into my mouth and she makes me dig down in the trash for the wrapper and then she makes me read the wrapper to her. Sugar, corn syrup, bleached wheat flour, dextrose, maltose, lactose, milk solids, do you even know this shit you're eating? she asks, shaking me, and when I start crying uncontrollably she marches me into the bathhouse and puts me up against the mirror and says, Look at yourself, just look at what you're doing to yourself. My face is all scrunched up and puffy and red and snotty. She sends me to bed without supper. Chardonay and Lisa are still grounded from the shoplifting.

When Lisa's not grounded anymore we go into Cotati looking for the disco parties she's always hearing about but which we never seem to find. We'll end up sitting on the curb in a shopping mall, some large empty place with no people in it. Lisa in a skimpy tube top with her boy shoulders poking out of it, sweating in the heat reflected from the pavement, her heels too big for her, wearing too much makeup. We walk back to the trailer park with the smell of car exhaust and the sound of our shoes on gravel and sometimes a little K.C. and the Sunshine Band or the Sylvers coming from a car radio going past.

I go back to watching traffic from the roof of the bathhouse, thinking about the space in between places and about how I've lived so many places I can't keep track of them. Already

I've forgotten about what it was like to live in Monte Rio or by the river.

Cotati is too bright and hot, all covered in pavement baking in the sun, the color and smell bleached out of everything, miles of parking lots and gas stations and self-storage units. Bright hot space divided by chain link fences and telephone poles. I walk against traffic to roller-skate along the paths of the university, empty for now, like a haunted place. An awning from a closed snack bar flaps in the wind, trash cans loll on their sides. A wall of closed windows shows me my reflection, small against all the empty space of the campus, lost and anonymous. Like the sound of the trucks crying down the highway, going places that aren't really there, driven by people I would never know, faceless people I'll never know, whose lives I can't imagine. The world is made up of spaces between places. This is what 1978 looks like to me. Being twelve years old. Maybe it's 1979.

Chapter 12

Hot Silence

I am hunkered down by the fire in the middle of an unbearably hot day, poking at the sticks to make them burn hotter at the edges so both of the pots on the fire will cook at once. One is a pot of brown rice for me and Helene and Tom and one is a pot of rice cream for Ki. The rice pot I don't open because it needs to gather steam to cook the rice. White starchy liquid bubbles fitfully up through the closed lid and runs down the side of the pot and gets burned black there. A crust of this burnt matter already covers the side of the pot. The other pot, with Ki's cereal, I have to open to stir it or the bottom will stick. I pull my sleeve down across my hand to make a pot holder and I set the lid of the pot on a rock that's my table rock, flat on top and with a little dip in it to hold the stirring spoon too. After minutes of watching it bubble, while sweat beads up on my forehead and drops darkly on the bamboo mat, I stir the ceral one more time and move it off the fire.

Ki is squatted down on her haunches a little way off, watching ants, a line of ants in the dirt that keeps her motionless for a long time. Her hair is almost blond from the sun and it falls over her browned face. I call her, Ki, rice cream, and she slowly straightens up and comes over to me for a bowl. Ground sesame and liquid aminos go into it, and her little wooden spoon. She eats her rice cream, sitting with the bowl between her legs on another bamboo mat spread on the ground. She sticks her hand in the bowl and licks it, the fat little fingers splayed wide.

There's some shade on the mats, sparse shade from a few oak trees. It's not really shade, just a darker version of sun. Everything is slow and hot and heavy, my thoughts and words, everything I do and think and see and say seems to happen in amber liquid air. Everything is quiet, a deep and vast quiet, except for the bugs, which hum and buzz in a pattern that starts and ends and starts and ends all day. Ki's spoon going from her bowl to her mouth, the bubbling starch, and the heat waves coming from the fire are the only things moving in this place. The fire burns without noticeable flame, just a white ash that shimmers on the logs. Ki's spoon scrapes the bowl and she puts them both down and looks at me and looks for Helene and then she just lays down on the mat and closes her eyes. We aren't living in the trailer park anymore.

Where we are is called Sugarloaf. It's a mountain somewhere in California but I don't know where. It's like I woke up and we were just here, and it's like I've always been here and even like there's no other place on earth.

When the rice pot isn't releasing liquid anymore that means the rice is almost done. When the liquid is gone I can take the lid off. Now I do that, pry up the lid with a stick, and also using the stick I poke a hole in the rice to see if there's any wet at the bottom. Wet at the bottom means it still has to cook more. I like the rice less cooked so it's more chewy, but Helene likes it fluffier and wetter. I don't know how Tom likes it. He never talks. When he does he answers in riddles, or he answers the question with another question. How do you like the rice cooked, Tom? I like it cooked.

Helene is off somewhere, wandering in the dry creek bed, maybe. Tom is meditating, sitting in more of the sparse not-quite-shade not far away. I can only see his back, bare, with his long ponytail hanging down the middle. His knobby knees stick out on either side of him, he's in the lotus position. His hands are most likely loosely cupped in his lap. His back is lined with bones, and he only wears loincloths lately. A loose wrapping of cotton around him. He still wears his amulets and bracelets and rings, though, so he still jingles when he moves. When he meditates he doesn't move, just becomes part of the stillness of the landscape. For hours. He sits by the dry creek for hours every day. I'm used to making as little noise as possible so I don't disturb his meditation. I don't ask him questions anymore. I don't think he likes kids.

Maybe Tom hears me take the lid off the rice pot, because he slowly raises his arms and brings his palms to his face. His shoulder blades move like wings made of thin brown wood. He breathes out deeply, I can hear this a long way off from where I'm sitting. He raises himself off the ground and walks over slowly, and he takes a bowl and hunkers by the fire next to me and gets some rice. Give thanks for rice, he says, and he turns and says, Thank you for the rice, and then he turns to the hills and says, Thank you for the rice. He lifts the bowl to his forehead and then sits cross-legged on the mat to eat. He raises the chopsticks slowly to his mouth and chews slowly and looks into nothing, somewhere on the mat.

The grass rustles a little. Helene in her skirts is moving through it. She must have been at the creek, because she slowly bends and places three red rocks and two white feathers at the base of the tree near us, and then she kneels by the pot and gets rice too. She's wearing shapeless gauze robes and they spread out around her on the ground. She tucks her legs underneath herself and leans over the pot, her hand crabbed over her rice bowl, her thumb inside the rim. She has to use her other hand to get the rice, but she has to put the spatula down to get her hair out of her eyes, and this seems to cause her an agitation, but a sleepy kind of agitation, meditative, like Tom. My mom is a Zen robot.

We eat mostly without speaking. This is our midafternoon meal, though we don't have set times to eat meals and there isn't any way to tell time anyway. I add more Braggs to my rice because rice alone tastes like basically nothing. There's no use in saying anything to Tom or Helene about the food. I eat because I have to and I eat what I have and I have even stopped thinking about food. I've stopped thinking about anything. I'm a bug in amber liquid, barely moving.

After eating I lie on the mat next to Ki and look up at the trees. If there was a breeze they might move and make a dry rustling but I don't think that's happened in a long time. Ki has her butt up in the air with her legs tucked under her and we sleep on into the afternoon. Maybe we've been here a month, maybe three days, maybe ten thousand years.

On another day here I lie on my stomach in a patch of dry grass with Ki, watching ants and beetles move up and down the dry stalks of burdock. We lie on our backs and watch a hawk moving far up in the sky. We sit up and watch the stones in the dry creek bed. After a while we get up and walk down to the creek, picking our way carefully over stickers and sharp stones. In the creek bed I pick up stones, put them to my ear, and put them back down. Helene told me a story, maybe from her book of Tibetan fables or Zen koans, about a prince under enchantment, trapped in the shape of a stone, waiting for someone to come and rescue him by listening to the sound of his voice coming from the stone. So for hours I pick up stones and put them to my ear. You could spend your life picking the stones up, listening, and putting them back down, and the stone you didn't pick up, the one just after the last one you listened to, might have the prince. This idea keeps me in the dry riverbed for hours, turning over one stone after another.

When I wander back to our cooking fire Tom and Helene are there, making a tea out of dried peyote buttons. They have spread a blanket out on the ground and after they make the tea, chanting over it, they meditate to contact the spirit of some peyote god. They drink the tea, and offer me some too, but it's so horribly bitter that I choke it out of my mouth and spit it into the grass.

Tom and Helene are trying to live spiritual lives. They are practicing mysticism. They are living up here on the mountain without a house or bathroom or running water or TV or radio or furniture or any food but rice to purify themselves. While they do this my boredom grows so huge it becomes an almost visible bubble surrounding not just me but everything around me as well. I live in an arid dome of silent unmoving boredom. The tireless mare roams the grass plains, Helene intones. Mystery upon mystery, manifold secrets.

Time passes and I can't say how much. At some point I am in the public bathroom that is about a mile from our camp, filling a plastic jug from a trickle of water that comes from the rusty spout. The bathroom is just a cinder block hut with a swinging door, a toilet with no water in it, and a sink. While the jug fills I hear a sound that I haven't heard in so long I have to think for a minute what it is, and then I realize it's a car or a truck coming up the road and stopping outside the bathroom. My brain is moving slow but I realize I'm trapped in the bathroom with no way out but the one door, and that the car is outside the door, and there are people in the car, and I'm scared to see them because I know what I must look like. This hits me right away, that I can't let people see me because I look like some kind of wild animal child. My hair is a ratted mess of tangles and probably burrs, my shorts are ragged corduroy cutoffs with strings hanging to my knees, my shirt used to be a stripey tee shirt but is now just a faded dishrag-looking thing that sags from my boney shoulders. My arms and legs are dry and scratched and have ground-in dirt. My scaly bare feet a have a kind of dry crust on top like alligator skin.

I come out of the bathroom, blinking in the white glare, and some people are getting out of a station wagon, a man and a woman and two kids, one my age, one younger. The woman and the man wear sunglasses and visors and she is wearing a pretty halter top of blue and yellow flowers. The girl my age is wearing a sundress with green and pink flowers. They are all fat and white and they stare at me like they're seeing a ghost or a monster or a rabid animal. I hurry on up the road, sloshing water from the jug onto my shorts and legs. The water leaves trails of wetness on my legs that make the dry skin stand out whitely, and then the water makes the alligator skin on my feet go red and itchy and later it cracks open and bleeds.

On another hot dry day after more time goes by Helene is tying up a bundle of things in an Indian bedspread, a blanket and a sweater and some pairs of my pants. Synchronicity rather than causality, she says, this is the essence of the Ching. You're going to New Mexico to be with Claude and Haud. I tossed the Ching about it. The cicada symphony rises and falls, not meaning anything, just waves of sound coming from the hills.

Chapter 13

The Essence of the I Ching

And then after this I was on a Greyhound bus, going to New Mexico. I have no memory of how this happened. I can invent that and it would be close to the truth or close to what might have happened.

The bus terminal booms, they all do, even the small ones. The ceiling is higher than it needs to be, room for all the worry of missed connections and the wonder of distance. Terminals boom and they click, too. Heels on polished floors, the janitor's cart with the loose wheel, the squeak and thump of luggage tossed to the floor. The sounds of buses coming and going is intermittent and not intrinsic to the terminal. The sound of the bus is only what you hear after you've been waiting and listening to the clicks and booms and squeaks and hisses of the terminal. The arrival and departure of the bus is incidental to the experience of waiting amidst the other sounds and movements. People sleeping and reading papers and eating potato chips from crinkling bags. People buying tickets and saying goodbye, leaving with worry and arriving with tiredness.

What I don't remember is what it was like to say goodbye to Tom and Helene. I did not see them again until I was twenty-one.

I can remember just a little of what it was like to leave Ki. I was troubled for a long time after leaving her. I felt I had abandoned her. I despaired for her, for my last image of her, standing on the curb at the bus station in her tattered pink poncho, holding Helene's hand and waving to me as the bus pulled away. I had dreams about Ki for years, desperate searches for her through jungles and abandoned cities. I did not see my sister again for several years and it was only then that I learned she'd been sent to live with her father not long after I was sent to live with mine. Ki didn't see Helene again until Ki was an adult.

Chapter 14

Edward Hopper's America

The trip on the bus from California to New Mexico was a piece of time that was separate from either place, a time traveling between other places that weren't places, really, just things I saw from the windows of the bus.

I wasn't afraid to be traveling alone, I knew what to do. Not lose my tickets, ask the drivers if I needed to change buses, and then ask the new drivers if I was on the right bus. Keep track of my bag. Stay near the bus at rest stops so it didn't leave without me. Stay where there was people.

Greyhound buses smell a certain way and they all smell the same, which is the smell of fake cherry from the bathroom deodorant they use. This smell pretty much ruined cherries for me and it stayed the same on every bus so it was like I was always on the same bus. Also a dry chemical smell of the seat covers, the smell of people smoking on the bus, the smell of exhaust and flat air conditioning that actually has a smell that is the absence of smell. On the bus the cold air was always a little too cold and the hot air was always a little too hot.

The windows were up a little too high for me, so I couldn't see out well unless I sat up really straight and craned my neck a little, which I did a lot. Mostly I sat up near the front and leaned my head against the window and watched the road unfurl up ahead, either from between the seats or from the very first seat which is right by the driver and a pretty exciting place to sit. Exciting in a relative kind of way. Best was to have a seat alone and curl up in it and sleep after I got tired of watching the road or other people or other cars.

On one of the buses I watched a man fooling with himself under a magazine that was open on his lap. He wore a big rumply army jacket and his hands were hidden in the folds but I could still tell what he was doing. He looked at the magazine for a while and then put his head back on the seat and moved his hands, and then he looked at the magazine some more and then moved his hands some more. I looked away. I looked back. He moved his hands faster and his shoulders heaved and his mouth moved. Finally he stiffened and sighed and then he was still and then he was snoring.

There was a lady I watched for a long time, too. She had long fingernails painted chocolate brown to match her lipstick, and hair so bright blond it looked like doll hair. She smoked and chewed gum and looked impatient and efficient, like she was maybe used to answering a phone, saying, Good afternoon law offices, and then, Would you hold please, while she looked at her fingernails and snapped her gum. Her jacket matched her skirt, which matched her purse, which matched her shoes.

Other people got on and off the bus. A skinny lady with three skinny kids, her face lined with worry, wearing a sheepskin jacket and cowgirl boots. She carried a plastic suitcase with a broken zipper and a diaper bag spilling Pampers and sweaters and cans of Tahitian Treat. One of the kids clutched a can of soda and she stared at me over the rim of her can as she drank in the aisle of the bus while the bus waited. She drank with both hands holding the can, her legs spread wide, her head thrown all the way back as she drained the last from the can. When she finished she had a ring of red around her mouth and she took a long breath and burped and tried to drink more but the can was empty. The skinny lady herded her and the two other kids along the aisle of the bus and settled them in, shoving her bags in the rack above her seat, and the bus pulled away, leaving a man, also skinny, also wearing a sheepskin jacket and boots, standing in the dust by an old truck. The man would go back to where they lived, I bet it would be a trailer, I bet it was a double wide, and he would sit down at the fake table and look at the table in the now-quiet trailer.

I watched cars pass us and I looked at cars we passed. You can see into the laps of people driving in cars beside buses. A big blue Impala, very long and wide, with a convertible top, pulling a small silver Airstream trailer. The man driving wore a cowboy hat, and from above all I could see of him was the brim of the hat and the swell of his stomach in his lap. He was driving with a woman who had piled-up black hair that didn't move an inch even in the wind of the open car. She wore a silver suit with sequins and bell-bottom pants and she had one leg hitched over the open window of the car with one high-heeled silver boot resting on the sill. When they pulled ahead of us, their license plate said USARODEO, and I thought about them parking their Airstream on the desert plain and setting up a card table under a pull-down awning. They would drink ice tea in plastic glasses and complain in slow voices about the heat.

About a million trucks passed us, their signs saying Piggly Wiggly and Safeway and Lucky and Albertsons. The Safeway sign is the yin and yang symbol of the west, Helene would say. Already I was forgetting about her, not thinking about her, letting her fade. Station wagons full of kids going on vacation with their parents passed us. Rows of legs lined up on seats, little kids on laps, coolers open in the back, spilling soda cans and bags of white bread and packages of hot dogs. Crumpled bags of chips stuffed between seats and under armrests. A mom's arm would reach behind her to flap at the air near some kid's head and I could almost hear her saying, You keep doing that and I'll smack you, you keep doing that and we'll stop the car right here and not even go to Disneyland or Six Flags or Marineworld or Grandma's. We passed VW Beetles full of hippies getting stoned, and fast cars zipping along with four or five girls in them, hair flying in the wind, and army jeeps with canvas on the tops flapping, and trucks carrying open loads of tomatoes and oranges and chickens losing feathers, people pulling horse trailers and people on motorcycles. All these different people out in the world going to all these different places, people and places I had forgotten about while I was up on Sugarloaf mountain with Tom and Helene. This was part of everything that was happening out in the world while we sat still up on the hill. I might have been still, but the world kept moving without me. It felt good to be watching the world move again.

We stopped at big cities and we stopped at small towns. I always woke up when we stopped because the feel and the sound of the bus would change, it would grind down through the gears and squeal and belch air and huff. Inside big bus terminals there were echoes of other buses coming and going and the smells of gas and oil. We went from the too-cold air of the bus to the too-hot air of the desert pavement during the day or the too-hot air of the heated bus at night to the too-cold air of the terminal. At night there was orange light in the terminals, grayish orange light from overhead like in tunnels. I would wake up with a start in a new place, a little disoriented, and look around me and then lean my head back on the seat again, swallowing to get the taste of sleep out of my mouth, blinking in the new light, rubbing my eyes, my ears popping with the pressure change if the doors had just opened suddenly. I might step out of the bus to stretch my legs, wander into the new terminal, stand with longing in front of the snack and soda machines.

In small towns the terminal might be a small building or it might be a parking lot or even just a stop on a corner, where people got on without buying a ticket and just paid the driver or bought a ticket at the next big stop. I might stand shivering in the chilly air of the desert night for a minute before going back on the bus. Quiet night air, the bus idling, a dog barking a long way off, other cars moving on the freeway. People traveling in the space between places.

For a while there were only small towns. Needles, maybe, or Mojave, or Grants. Towns with just one long main street with a few side streets branching off. A drugstore, a gas station, a bar, a diner, houses with porches, all of weathered wood and peeling paint. A garage wall patched with flattened tin cans nailed to the splintered wood, tar paper peeling in strips, a faded Pegasus on the side of a gas station. Something about these towns, all dusty in the heat of day with no one around, or quiet under the big sky at night, was like being somewhere after a war with no people left alive. No bodies lying around but I got the feeling the people were all gone. Wiped out by a plague or carried off by aliens or fallen to a sleeping sickness. Tired towns, empty and lonely, but peaceful, edged with the gold of late-afternoon sun, long horizontal shadows from a can lying on its side.

And for a long time there was only desert. The road and the land were dry and flat and empty. The desert isn't dead but it sure looks that way from the window of a Greyhound bus, because whatever happens in the desert, it happens slow. No rain in the desert, but the ghost of rain, because you can't be in the desert without thinking about rain. The bus threw long shadows on the road as the day moved into afternoon, the shadow sliding over clumps of sagebrush and juniper and dry weeds, cactus. The freeways were lined with cans bleached white by the sun, brown and green bottles, scraps of tires. I watched these remains go by, thinking that they were things not connected to anything else, no place and no feelings and no life attached to them, lying under the big empty sky. Day after day the sun would rise and cross the sky over these bottles and cans and tires and tatters of cloth and curling shoes and their shadows would stretch across the ground and night would come again and they would just lie there, unmoving, no longer connected to the land of the living, not even waiting for someone to come along and pick them up and turn them over.

I know that America is a huge place and full of people, all the kinds of places and people you can imagine, but what I was thinking inside the Greyhound bus was that America is just one long highway baking quietly in the sun and waiting for the cars it bears. America from the bus felt like all space, all distance, and this made me feel empty inside and a little tired, my mind wiped clean, just waiting for the next thing to happen, waiting for the next place I would be.

Chapter 15

We're ALL Barefoot!

Well, look at this. It's Clank and Honk, together again in New Mexico. Larry is saying this, bent over a table made out of an old telephone-cable spool. He's leaning into a pool of light cast by a kerosene lamp, trying to see a splinter in his thumb. I'm going to get this damn splinter out so it doesn't work its way into my bloodstream and go to my brain and turn me into a mutant. He makes a mutant face at Haud and looks back at his thumb. I'm getting this sucker out and then I'm going to roll a fat doobie. He takes a long pull out of a bottle of Miller High Life, his Adam's apple bobbing up and down and his throat going grk grk grk, and calls, Carol where are the tweezers? Carol calls back in her nasally whine, Can't you find them yourself? Do I have to do everything? Oh, she's cracked, Larry mutters. The lamp throws flickering shadows around the big room, the light just barely reaching the wooden beams of the ceiling and making a pale circle on the dirt floor.

Haud and I are sitting on the floor playing Chinese checkers. It's hard to tell the color of the marbles in the lamplight and I'm getting blue mixed up with green and Haud is winning. I say, Let's switch to real checkers and Haud says, You're just a sore loser.

You kids stop bickering. Who wants some apple juice? Carol comes from the part of the room called the kitchen, where the big woodstove and big wood cupboard are, with three chipped blue enamel mugs of apple juice. Don't forget to brush afterwards, she says, also handing us each a licorice twig. The apple juice is the sweet homemade kind that's cloudy, and it's cold from being outside in the night air. Carol and Larry are always chewing licorice twigs to keep their teeth and gums healthy. Carol is forever working the twig around her big front teeth and talking past it at the same time. Larry always calls us Clank and Honk. When you brush your teeth go ahead and get into bed, it's nine o'clock, Carol says, leaning against the wall and rubbing the twig across her teeth. We've got plenty of work to do tomorrow.

Carol and Larry are friends of Claude's and we're staying at their house in Ojo Sarco, which is in New Mexico, until Claude is finished with a job he's doing, something with a backhoe. He has a backhoe and he's been working down the road digging into a hillside. Earlier today he showed us the hole he tore out of the hill above the road. The blades had sliced into the earth and left a square hole that trailed tree roots and spilled pink dirt and chunks of sandstone down into the road. A school is going to go here, Claude said. We're going to build a free school right here above the road for all the Sarco kids to go to. He was wearing a bandanna around his head to keep the sweat from going in his eyes and he was bare-chested and leaning on the backhoe, one hand on it all the time like it would walk away if he weren't touching it. Haud ran around the backhoe, looking at it from all sides, and I peered into the cab and said, Wow do you keep from falling out? There's no door.

Carol and Larry live down the road from Claude's house in Ojo Sarco. They live in an old house that was falling down and which they're taking apart and putting back together, fixing it up, which supposedly Claude is doing too, to his house. Carol and Larry are living in the house while they work on it, and we're helping them. Their house is adobe, which most of the houses around here are made of. Adobe is mud brick, and you can make the bricks yourself. Carol and Larry say they're getting back to the land.

In the morning, after a breakfast of granola and goat's milk from Preacher's goats down the road, only he's not really a preacher, we go right to work making adobe bricks to fix Carol and Larry's house. There's a big pit in the yard near the house where we make them. During the night the pit in the ground has dried out, so we drag the garden hose over and turn it on and fill the pit partway with water. Then we take shovels and picks and hoes and we stomp around in the pit making mud. Then we add straw and sand. Larry climbs down into the pit in his rubber boots and rolls some of the mud between his thumb and finger and says, Looks good. At one end of the pit the ground slopes up gradually, and down this slope he rolls a wheelbarrow, which us kids slop full of the mud. Larry huffs the wheelbarrow up out of the pit and Carol takes it and wheels it to the forms. The forms are laid out flat on the ground, rows and rows of wooden rectangles, big rectangles made up of twelve smaller rectangles. Carol slops the forms full of mud from the wheelbarrow and Haud and I run behind her, shaking the forms to make the mud settle in without air pockets. While we do this Larry makes more mud in the pit, and the pit gets bigger and bigger, and more and more forms are laid out on the ground with adobes drying in them. We're all hot and dirty and spattered with mud. Haud has mud in his hair and Larry and Carol each have mud swiped across their foreheads from their habit of brushing their long hair out of their eyes. Larry wears his rubber boots and holey jeans and a plaid shirt bleached almost white by being washed and then dried on the line in the sun. Carol wears a raggedy purple halter top and cutoffs and work boots over heavy wool socks in mismatched colors, and her arms and shoulders are strong and her legs are hairy and brown. She has her hair tucked into a cowboy hat and a little mud spattered on her glasses, too. Me and Haud are barefooted and Haud isn't wearing a shirt and his tiny spare tire jiggles as he runs. I have a shirt with purple butterflies on it which is an old one of Carol's and is way too big but pretty, and a little necklace of shells tied together. Both of our hair is long and ratty.

We shake forms for half the day behind Carol, and then Carol checks to see if the bricks are drying evenly in the sun without cracking. When the bricks dry enough the sides pull away from the forms and the forms can be lifted off the bricks, and then the bricks have to dry more. Stacking the bricks after they're dried is the hardest part. They're heavy and scratchy and rough and they dig into the meat of my arms when I carry them. The pile of dry bricks is now almost too high to reach up onto, and I think maybe we get to stop now. Larry says, Okay now you kids start another row on the ground. You kids got soft in California. We start to whine and Carol says finish that row and then go wash up in the ditch and we'll eat.

In the cool dimness of the house she sets a pot of water to boil on the little propane stove that they have along with the woodstove. The wood one is too hot for the summer and takes too long to light. Go out into the garden and get some ears of corn, she says, and a few ripe tomatoes and a cucumber too, and some bigger lettuce leaves. I run out of the house across the dirt yard, past the woodpile and chopping block, stepping light and fast over the chips so I don't come down hard on a knot or a sharp piece, my arms and legs wet from the ditch and red with scratches from the bricks. I hiss at the cat, sitting on the woodpile waiting for mice, which hisses back, and I run along the board that crosses the ditch, sunlight sparkling off the water, and I hop through a hole in the clump of plum trees. In the garden, I stop to run my thumb across a basil leaf and smell it, sunlight warming my back. The garden smells so good in the sun.

I make a bowl out of my shirt bottom and fill it with ears of corn and a cucumber and three fat tomatoes and a bunch of lettuce leaves, and I take a few peas for the fun of popping them open. On the porch I strip the ears and I wash the lettuce in a bowl of water and I take the stems off the cucumber and shell the peas. We have salad with a dressing of safflower oil and tamari and brewers' yeast, and we eat the corn with soy margarine. We have tortillas spread with oil and mungbean sprouts from the jar on the windowsill.

I've been at Carol and Larry's for a little while, a few weeks maybe. When the Greyhound bus pulled into Española, which is the next biggest town near Ojo Sarco, Carol picked me up and we drove up the valley to the house. I've been to Ojo Sarco before, way before, when I was five and Claude first moved here. As we drove up I looked for things I remembered, but we came the back way, which is mostly just trees and brush and mesas and the dirt road, no landmarks, nothing to really show that time has passed.

When we pulled into Carol and Larry's driveway, Haud jumped on me before I could even get the gate open. He was all wiggling like a puppy, a wide grin on his face like he almost even missed me. We started to wrestle right away and he said, I got bigger, see, I'm almost bigger than you now. He stood up tall, panting, and his hair was even longer and wilder than before, and his feet were bare and his shorts were hanging off his butt and his stomach showed between his shirt and his shorts. He said, Me and Larry are fixing a dirt bike and he lets me sit on it and I'm going to ride it. He told me all about Carol and Larry's house and about the neighbor kids. They were there, three of them, standing under the plum trees and watching us come in. I was scared to meet them and went into the house right away.

Carol and Larry showed me the house and what they were doing to it and where I would sleep. Their house has running water but no electricity inside and no toilet or bathroom. Almost none of the houses in Ojo Sarco have toilets. The floor is half dirt and half wood. On the dirt part, which is packed down hard and swept every day and doesn't seem like it's dirty even though it's a dirt floor, is the kitchen, which also has a greenhouse. There is a wooden part where the beds are, a futon on the floor covered in homemade quilts for Carol and Larry and sleeping bags on yoga mats for me and Haud. You can put those mats under the futon during the day, Carol said, and I said okay. Here's our new window seat, Larry said, and it was covered in a flowery cushion. That's a nice place to watch the sunrise, Carol said. There was a Mason jar of wildflowers on the spool table, yarrow and Indian paintbrush and sunflowers, and strings of chiles and braided garlic and onions hanging over the stove. The house is low and a little dark, which keeps it cool all day, and dusty, but way better than a tent.

There's someone who wants to meet you, Carol said, putting some groceries away and showing me where to dump my bag. I scuffed my bare toes in the dirt and crossed my arms over my chest and wouldn't go outside, but I moved closer to the door to see out of it. I hung on the door for a minute, looking outside a little at a time. There was a big yellow dog with a gray snout sitting on its rump on the porch, and a boy sitting on the chopping block, and a girl sitting quietly on one of Carol's broken chairs, the wicker one, holding a littler girl in her lap. I caught just a glimpse of their big dark eyes and dark hair, and a couple more kids out in the yard, all waiting for me to come out. That's Annabelle, Larry said, from where he was looking for something in a toolbox. He pulled a wrench out and threw it on the floor where it hit with a soft *thumfp*. They're nice kids and they've been looking forward to you coming. I peeked outside again and Annabelle wasn't wearing any shoes either. I looked at my own bare feet. I looked at Carol. I went outside.

Annabelle stood up from the chair and said hi shyly. She had straight black hair that hung in bangs in her eyes a little, and she brushed the hairs out of her eyes and pushed the little girl gently off her lap and stood up. I'm Annabelle, she said. This is Dolores, we call her Dodie, and that's Geraldine and Gerald and over there is Roger. Haud was already wrestling with Gerald. Roger waved at me a little. Roger's thirteen, Annabelle's twelve, Gerald and Geraldine are nine, and Dodie is four. I said, We're ALL barefoot! and Annabelle said, Who needs shoes in summer? and we went to go eat plums from the trees and float leaf boats in the ditch.

Now I play with Roger and Annabelle and Geraldine and Gerald and Dodie every day. They live next door to Carol and Larry, in a house spackled the same dirty pink and white as Carol and Larry's, only theirs isn't falling apart or being worked on, it sits square and regular in a bare dirt yard that their grandma sweeps every day. Carol and Larry's yard has stuff all over it, the woodpile, different cars and trucks that Larry either drives or uses for parts for the ones that do drive, the dirt bike he's fixing, the clothesline, the outhouse, piles of lumber, the adobes we're making, and a washing machine. The washing machine is the kind that swishes the clothes around in a big open drum and you can watch, the kind where you have to pull the wet clothes through a pair of rollers to wring them dry. Annabelle's house sits way back from the road, Carol and Larry's sits right near the road, which is lined with sage and juniper and scrubby dried-looking brush and weeds that grow up through the barbed-wire fence.

Ojo Sarco, this town, it's not even a town, doesn't have streets or stoplights or even stop signs, it's just a wide valley with a dirt road running along either side. Ojo Sarco is in the northern part of New Mexico, not very far from Santa Fe, maybe an hour, and not very far from Taos, maybe an hour. Albuquerque is an hour and a half away to the south. I always remember it being just about the same, the same old adobe farmhouses, rectangle-shaped with small windows and tin roofs, spackled with plaster or whitewash or cement, or some just mud. Some trailer houses, plenty of falling-down sheds and melting-in adobe shacks and funny old one-room houses that no one lives in anymore. In almost every yard there's a mean dog that comes out to the road to bark when you go by, and in almost every yard there's a rusty pickup truck or a tractor or a faded old car with huge fins and hanging-off doors, sitting on flat tires. Cottonwoods line the creek that runs between the two roads, tall old trees that release tufts of cottony fiber into the air in the last part of summer, so the trees float in thin clouds of soft drifty white. The houses look like they are growing out of the ground, because when it rains here it rains hard and dirt spatters from the ground up the sides of the houses.

Almost every day we help Carol and Larry with the adobes for a while and then we eat and then we play with Roger and Annabelle and Gerald and Geraldine and Dodie and the big old yellow dog. We help them with their chores when they come home from school. I'll look out the window from where I'm sitting on the window seat and the school bus comes and the kids get off, and then in a minute I'll see the girls walking out of the house with a basket of clean wash to hang on the line or a tin pail for picking alfalfa for the chickens. Roger will go out to chop wood and Gerald helps him pick up chips for kindling. We hang up clothes and sheets on the clothesline and Gerald and Roger teach me words in Spanish. I know some swear words and I ask them, What's *chignon*, and the girls giggle and Geraldine says, that's a badword. Roger says, It's like fucker. Then what's *chingonada*, I ask, and Annabelle claps her hands over Dodie's ears and Roger shrugs and says, Fucked. Annabelle picks up a stick and chases Roger with it and they're laughing and the dog is trying to jump around them but he's too old and finally he sits back down, his wagging tail making a track in the dirt.

On the other side of the road from Carol and Larry's and just around a bend, there's Mamacita's house. Mamacita's house is one of the things about New Mexico that never changes. It's spackled the same funny colors as Carol and Larry's and it has a tin roof and a porch all the way around. It sits low and long on a small rise above the road, with one straggly tree near it, in a yard worn smooth and hard by hundreds of kids' feet and dogs' feet and the feet of Mamacita's husband and brothers and sisters and sons and cousins and daughters.

Mamacita is tiny and round and white-haired and she never ever sits down. I go into her house to buy milk from her cows or to take her some vegetables from the garden and she will be at the stove spooning up beans or flipping tortillas or washing dishes or giving a glass of milk to one of the kids or ironing someone's clothes or sometimes just standing at the sink talking really fast in Spanish with one hand waving in the air and another at her hip. Carol says that woman cooks all day. She makes the first breakfast for Pedro before dawn, and when she finishes the last breakfast for Mercy it's time to make lunch for Levi and Rogelio coming in from their night shifts at Los Alamos, and when they finish their lunch it's time to make dinner for the grandkids coming home from school. In Mamacita's kitchen the counter tops are worn white from scrubbing and the floor is worn smooth in a trail from the fridge to the stove to the sink. Mamacita doesn't have a dirt floor, she would never stand for that. The floors are all cement and are always swept clean without a speck of dirt anywhere, and the beds are covered in yellow spreads worn almost through in spots. There is flowered wallpaper in a pattern she must have got from the general store in Dixon thirty years ago, Carol says she's been here her whole life. Nothing on the walls but pictures of a blond Jesus, our lady of Guadalupe, and graduation pictures of all her grown kids.

Carol says go bring Mamacita some zucchini, it's taking over the garden, and so I trudge up the road and up the little hill to the kitchen door, and I hang there a minute, my arms full of ridiculously big zucchini, looking in. There's someone eating at the table, his arms around his plate and his face bent over it. There is Mercy talking to Mamacita in fast Spanish, Mercy in jeans ironed so much the crease shows pure white. There are two or three nephews and nieces and grandkids maybe seven or eight or nine years old, sitting at the table drinking sodas out of plastic cups. The kids stare at me, the youngest one's mouth an "o" of surprise. My feet are bare and dirty and I put one muddy foot on top of the other to hide my feet. The dusty squashes are almost bigger than me and absurd in the clean kitchen where everything is scrubbed clean and everything is neat and straight. I know my hair is tangled and there are strings hanging off my cutoffs and I've been wearing the same purple shirt that Carol gave me for days. The boys are wearing short pants, cuffed, and shoes with socks, white ironed shirts, and even belts.

The man who is eating looks up from his plate, chewing slowly, and he looks at his son, and says, Don't stare, how would you like it if I stared at you like that? Two of the kids look down into their sodas quickly and take gulps of soda, and one keeps looking at me. The man says, Do you want me to have to take my belt off? and he half rises from his chair and reaches for his belt and the boy looks down at the table and swings his legs fast underneath it. Mercy takes the squash and Mamacita gives me a gallon of milk in a glass jar and I walk down the drive carefully, holding the cold glass against my chest.

When Roger and Annabelle come home we play kick the can in the road. Hardly any cars come and when they do we stand off to the side of the road and watch them. Old pickups that rattle with the back full of cans or tools and a big dog standing up and barking furiously at us as the truck goes by. Someone driving in a cowboy hat pulled low over his eyes and he lifts two fingers off the steering wheel at us and we wave back. The dust of the road is soft and we all scatter through it, playing and yelling. The New Mexico sky is the deepest possible blue, the hills are reddish brown and when we go down to the creek to put our dirty feet in the ditch everything is green and cool and wet.

Roger and Annabelle's dad comes home from work and we all run behind the truck as it pulls into the yard. He brings them sodas from the post office, which is the only store in the whole valley. We each get a cold can of Nehi and I choose grape, and the can sweats translucent purple drops. He works at Los Alamos and has to leave for work at five in the morning. He's a big man and quiet like Roger and Gerald are. He has handlebar mustaches and he eases himself stiffly out of the truck and says, Go help your mother *muchachos*. Their mom comes out of the house and she hands a pail to Annabelle. Come pick lamb's-quarter with us? Annabelle asks, squinting, shading her eyes against the afternoon sun with one hand, the other hand holding the bucket. We walk into the field below the house with Dodie following us, leaving a trail through the alfalfa, which is up to our knees and covered in small purple flowers. We look for lamb's-quarter in the alfalfa, it grows wild all over, and when we've filled the bucket I say, That should be enough for those chickens. Annabelle looks down at her feet and says, with a kind of still look on her face, No, we eat them. They're like spinach. She's waiting to see if I say anything like eewww you eat weeds? but I don't. Me and Haud go back to Carol and Larry's when Annabelle's mom calls supper. Carol said not to eat at Roger and Annabelle's house because they don't need two extra mouths to feed.

When we're not working on the house, Carol does yoga and Larry works on the dirt bike or on one of his trucks. Haud watches him, sitting near him in the dirt and handing him tools while Larry swears. This bitch needs a whole new carburetor, we might as well go on over to Felix's. Felix has parts for everything. We climb into the truck that works and it's Haud's turn to open the gate and then close it behind us, and we take off in a cloud of dust.

Felix lives down the road in a ramshackle house set way back from the road in a ghost parking lot full as the eye can see with junked cars and trucks. They line the slope like a rusted army. Three mean dogs bark at us from the porch with their hair all standing up. Felix comes out onto the porch, a leathery man bent over, wearing baggy jeans that are crusted with motor oil and a red-checked shirt and a cowboy hat crushed from his dirty hands. He yells at the dogs, and Haud and Larry go off to look for parts and I go into Felix's house. Inside, the walls are covered with flattened soda and coffee cans that have been nailed to the walls. There's a greasy table leaning over with stuff all over it, bolts and nuts and tins of screws and half a loaf of Wonder bread and a tin of sardines. There are shelves all the way up the walls, and the shelves are lined with shoe boxes and cans and cartons of more parts and junk. The house has an oily smell and a gasoline smell and the smell of an old man living by himself.

Felix sits on the porch and I can see him outside the door, just the shape of one of his knees in dirty jeans poking out from his chair. A dog settles in the doorway, watching me with his ragged head on his crossed paws, his nose twitching at flies. Outside I can hear Haud and Larry calling to each other faintly and then I hear thunder, more clearly and closer than their voices. The dog picks his head up at the thunder and then all three dogs are watching over the hills. Larry comes onto the porch with his smudged hands all full of parts and he gives Felix some money and they talk for a little while, about Felix's son who's in the army at Fort Dix, what a dry summer it's been, how maybe it'll finally rain if this storm settles in.

Larry says, We might as well go on up to the post office, back into the truck. Me and Haud ask, Can we stand in the back? We clamber up over the tailgate and stand behind the roof of the cab, holding on to the ridge that runs around the top. Larry drives fast as we bump over the road, leaving a cloud of dust hanging behind·us. We pass the old barn that I use as my best landmark. Each time I'm in Ojo Sarco it's falling a little farther over to one side, slanting closer to the ground, loose boards jutting out at weird angles, the windows dark and empty like staring eyeholes. Someday it's going to be just about horizontal, that barn. I watch for this barn because its decay is a process that can be measured over time. It is always in the same place and I can return to it and see the change, and this is not true for anything else in my life. There isn't even a doorway with marks for my height.

　　We pass Rodger Dodger's, the church, the one streetlight in the whole valley, the fork in the road where you can take the back way out to the highway, and we cross the wooden bridge over the creek. We pass Jim and Shirley's and the hole Claude has dug in the side of the hill where he said there would be a school. The hole is beginning to crumble back into itself, and tree roots dangle weirdly from the cut earth. We pass Claude's house and I can see his Army jeep and a whole lot of other broken down cars and trucks but not his flatbed dump truck or the backhoe. We go up the one really big hill and fly around the bend and then there's one long stretch and then there's the post office.

The post office is also the gas station. You can get your mail, chat with the mail lady, buy candy and cigarettes and gum and soda and motor oil and a fishing permit and a tamale out of a crockpot on the counter. Larry says we can have sodas but not to tell Carol and I pick strawberry and I take mine out to the porch while Larry pumps gas and Haud stands on the running board getting in the way.

From this rise in the road where the post office is you can see all the way across the valley and a whole big patch of sky. The sky is low and purple and here where we are and down below in the valley there are forks of lightning licking the tops of the mesas. Beyond the mesas the valley opens out into towering sandstone cliffs and gorges eaten into tortured shapes, which are red and brown and yellow and gilded with the last rays of afternoon sun that are slanting below the boiling purple towers of clouds. The New Mexico sky is funny this way. It's such a big sky, there can be rain, clouds, lightning, and clear blue sky all at once. The air has a tremendously wonderful smell, the smell of dust and sage juniper and hot earth waiting for rain. Rain in the desert is a celebration, everything waiting for it and welcoming it.

We drive back down the valley with the first few fat drops splatting on the windshield and making a loud sound on the roof of the truck and an audible *thump* on the road, sending up little poofs of dust each time a drop hits. There are great bursts of beautiful smell coming in the open truck windows and there is something like joy knocking around in my chest. We make it to the house just before the sky really opens up, and we listen to rain on the roof and play checkers.

Summer is almost fall now. Overripe plums drop from the trees onto an old camper shell sitting on the ground where me and Annabelle are guiltily but happily looking through a *Playboy* we found. We're looking at pictures of ladies and reading the comics. Haud and Gerald are playing war, hunkered down behind the woodpile and the outhouse going, Pew pew pew I got you sucker die die. Gerald dies with horrible gurgly moans. Annabelle shuts the magazine quick when Geraldine pops into the camper and says we have to help peel chiles.

Annabelle's house has a porch all around it and a linoleum and cement floor and a woodstove like Mamacita's. There are three tiny bedrooms so small that the beds take up all the space, each bed caving in the middle and neatly made with the spreads tucked tightly at the corners. The walls in the bedrooms are covered in wallpaper samples, each a different rectangle of pink flowers or green leaves or red checks or yellow stripes.

Annabelle's mom and grandmother are roasting chiles on the woodstove. There's a big burlap sack of green chiles leaning in the corner and the grandma takes a handful and throws them on top of the stove, where they hiss and swell and turn brown and the skin starts to peel away. When the skin cracks and curls she uses an oven mitt to take the done chiles and she throws them in a huge enamel bowl sitting on the table. The kitchen is hot and close with the smell of roasting chiles. Annabelle and I together take the bowl of chiles onto the porch and sit in chairs with the bowl between us, and we peel chiles all afternoon into the warm dusk. Her mom gives us peeled chiles wrapped in a tortilla which she baked on the stove, soft and hot and bubbled brown and rich with lard.

On a day that Carol says is harvest day the four of us drive down the dirt road until it turns back into asphalt and then we're out of the valley and we're in Dixon, which is a tiny town along the Embudo River. We go fast over the dip in the road and whoop when the truck goes into the air a little, and we turn off the road into a little cluster of hippie houses that everyone calls Cañoncito. The houses are all crazy-shaped, there's a dome and a kiva and a tower and lean-tos, and someone is always adding something to it. This time some long-haired men and women in crazy skirts and no shirts are mudding ceramic-tile mosaic onto the walls of the tower.

All afternoon with baskets we help pick apples and tomatoes and squash and beans and corn, laying out basket after basket in the big community kitchen. In the field hippies in straw hats and sombreros and neckerchiefs and no shirts and sometimes no clothes at all are bringing baskets of apples to the press to make cider or cooking big pots of tomato sauce over an open fire for canning. Then the grownups smoke pot and gossip while the kids lay on the wooden bridge watching for garter snakes and waterskeeters. By the creek there are horsetails and osha and mint and Queen Anne's lace and small apple trees with sour fruit because they've gone wild. Back to the land, Larry says, exhaling a huge cloud of pot smoke. We moved to Ojo Sarco to get back to the land. We take a crate of tomatoes and beans and corn and a jug of cider and an ounce of pot for Carol and Larry and get back in the truck and drive to the general store in Dixon.

Dixon is a tiny town but still bigger than Ojo Sarco. There's paved roads and a stop sign and a school I went to one time for a little while until I fell off the merry-go-round and scraped myself really badly and then didn't want to go anymore. All the houses are old and set low to the ground and painted the colors of New Mexico, turquoise and sage green and the purple of the clouds and the pink of the sandstone. Fat old Chevy trucks with wooden slats on the back and square old Fords going to rust sit in all the driveways. There are a few leaning sheds and outhouses and barns with Coca-Cola and Nehi and Skoal signs nailed to them. There is a little lazy movement here and there, a dog crossing the road, an old Chicana woman sitting on a porch wrapped in a shawl, rocking.

At the general store we buy chicken wire and chicken feed and tar paper and canning lids, and we drive back up the valley leaving another long cloud of dust to settle behind us. I hang my head out of the window and watch cactus and sage and anthills and sunflowers flash past us, and Haud shoots imaginary rabbits. Maybe I'll make spaghetti with all these fresh tomatoes, Carol says, chewing on a licorice stick. Haudie, don't lean so far out of the window or you'll fall out, and then we'll just leave you there. Yeah, the coyotes will eat you, Larry cackles.

Chapter 16

Dorothea Lange

We're leaving Carol and Larry's and we're going to Claude's house now. One afternoon Larry was chopping weeds along the side of the road in front of the house and me and Haud were helping him stack them and haul them to the compost pile when Claude drove by. Claude slowed down and reversed and backed up, the engine whining, and he stuck his head out of the high cab of the dump truck and said, Well hi there. Larry how's it going, man? and Larry said, Fine, man, fine. When you gonna pick up Clank and Honk? Claude took a long drag from his cigarette, and with smoke coming out of his nostrils and the afternoon sun glinting off his eyeglasses, he said, Drop 'em on by tomorrow afternoon. Okay kids, let's finish this up, Larry said. Carol baked us a carob cake in the oven of the woodstove that night and we had a few final games of checkers.

In the morning I'm restless and edgy. Carol and Larry's house is already gone to me, it's already the last place I was at instead of a place I'm still at. I help her sweep the dirt floors and pick up eggs from the chickens and weed the garden and wash some clothes in the washing machine in the yard. In the afternoon we stuff our few things into bags and pile into the car and drive down the road, past Mamacita's and Felix's and the leaning barn and the fork in the road near the church and over the wooden bridge and around the bend, past Jim and Shirley's, and we pull into Claude's driveway.

The house isn't really Claude's, it's Lore's. Lore's real name is Hannelore but no one calls her that, just Lore, like Laurie. Lore is Claude's mom and our grandmother. I don't know her well. She lives in Las Vegas, in Nevada. When Claude first came to Ojo Sarco he thought it was so great that he convinced Lore into buying this house and the fields around it, and now Claude lives here and is supposed to be fixing it up.

The house is a more solid version of Carol and Larry's, one story with an attic and a peaked tin roof, spackled yellow and green. It's not falling apart as much as Carol and Larry's, not hardly at all. It sits right off the road in a small apple orchard with the ditch down below it and a little outhouse across the ditch, and below that the creek.

Larry drives his battered Volvo carefully into the driveway, which is steep and gravelly, and we all get out. Haud and I throw our bags at the back door, which is locked, and we run around to the front of the house calling, Claude! Claude! The door at the front of the house, looking out over the fields and down into the creek, is open and a slice of daylight slanting across the dirt floor into the kitchen turns the rest of the room into a dark cave. I step in and know that no one is there. On the floor there are some empty cat food cans with dried crust at the bottom and one chair leans drunkenly against the wall, which is green in part but mostly just bare adobe where the plaster is falling away. The table in the kitchen, another telephone-cable spool, is covered in papers and full ashtrays. I go through the kitchen and then quickly through the rest of the house. It smells like dust and old clothes and motor oil, like Felix's.

When I walk back outside Carol and Larry are standing in the yard, both with a certain kind of look on their faces that is careful to have no look. Carol has her arms crossed and she's staring out across the field, which is bare except for burdock and ragweed and thistle. Her eyes are invisible behind her dark glasses. Larry has his lips pursed in a tuneless whistle and is picking his way aimlessly around the warped boards and melting cardboard boxes and rusty pans in the yard. He says, without looking at us, You kids going to be okay? and turns back to the car without waiting for an answer. Carol follows him, not saying anything. I feel almost frantic with the need to tell them I'm sorry the house is a mess and that Claude's not there and it's not my fault. Down somewhere at the bottom of my chest is the thing I can't let myself think, which is please don't leave us here, followed by, please leave so you can't see this anymore. Carol gives me a quick hug and gets in the car and starts chewing on her fingernail, looking out of the windshield at nothing while Larry reverses up the drive looking backwards over his shoulder to see the road. When they're gone there's just a cloud of dust and the faint sound of the car climbing up the hill.

Haud has his head poked into the rusted remains of a woodstove. Next door I hear Mal's door slam. We look at each other. Let's go over to Mal's. We pick our way carefully past a broken windshield leaning against the fence and slide through a hole in the boards. Mal used to be Claude's old lady and she's our brother Random's mom. She and Claude came to Ojo Sarco together when I was five and Haud was three and Random wasn't born yet. She has a house right next door.

Around the side of Mal's house we find her, working in the garden, bent over hoeing squash. She has strong hairy brown legs like Carol's and she's wearing a stained tennis visor to keep the sun out of her eyes, and sweat darkens the back of her tee shirt. Hi Clanie, she says. I'm mulching here. Hey Random, your long-lost sister and brother are here. She wipes some sweat from her face and keeps hoeing. Her garden is full of hugely lush green mounds of squash and chard and kale, and thick bright lines of marigolds and zinnias snake their way through the vegetables. At the edges are tall stands of sunflowers and I know that behind the sunflowers there will be a few pot plants, as big as trees in this dirt that she's been composting and mulching and hoeing since she moved here, maybe like six years ago.

Random comes crawling on his hands and knees around the side of the house, pushing a toy tractor in front of him, going Beep beep beep. Haud runs over to Random and they're squatting in the dirt pushing trucks and tractors and cars. Back up now, okay hode it, okay let's make a ditch here for the cars to get stuck in so the trucks can pull them out.

Random is four or maybe five. His hair is yellow blond, straight and stubby as straw, and his cheeks are bright red and ruddy and round like apples. His chubby arms and legs are scratched and dry like ours. He's wearing a pair of swimming goggles and nothing else and his peter dangles between his legs as he gets on all fours to dig in the ground. His hair sticks up in all directions and he smiles at me through gobs of drool and shows me a birdhouse he nailed together out of scraps of wood, and he shows me the hammock strung between two pear trees. While Haud pushes the trucks around in the dirt Random goes around the back of the house and comes back with a cat, which he dumps on the ground and then holds down with one grubby fat hand, the thumb of the other hand in his mouth. This is Kwikwi, he says around his thumb, squashing Kwikwi into the ground and petting her fur the wrong way. Her fur is as messy as Random's hair and Mal, coming up from the garden and wiping her hands on her shorts, says, Random's tough on cats.

In the house Random squats on the kitchen floor, petting Kwikwi with honey on his hands after showing me the jars that he and Mal collected from their beehives. He comes to wedge himself in the crook between Mal's knees while she tries to braid garlic from the garden, and with one hand on her knee he twists the other hand through his hair, absently worrying a hunk of it over and over again. Mal gently untwists his hand from his hair and takes his thumb from his mouth while she asks me about California. She looks muscly and tough like a mountain lady, doing all her own work. I haven't seen her in a long time, not since Random was born, and don't really know what to say, but I'm glad she's here next door to Claude's empty house.

When I lived here with Mal when she and Claude were still together it looked more like Claude's house does now, peeling plaster and dirt floors and the roof coming apart. Claude made me a loft in the kitchen and I climbed in and out of it all winter, it stayed warm even when it snowed. That was the first time I saw snow, and that spring Haud wore a pair of footed pajamas around for two months, refusing to take them off. It was also that spring that I got lice and had to have all my hair cut off, and like Haud, I would only wear one thing for months, which was a pink dress so no one would think I was a boy with my short hair.

Mal makes us all some sun tea with mint from the garden and the honey from her hives, which are past the chicken coop at the side of the house. Mal's house was the very first one I lived in when we came to Ojo Sarco when I was five. It just had two rooms painted turquoise green, and on our first day here we ate white bread and raspberry jam sandwiches in her blue-green house. There was straw falling from the ceiling because that's how houses are made here, with straw in the ceiling between the little logs and the big ones. Like every adobe house in this valley, the walls are two feet thick and the windows are low to the floor. Seeing her house now, it looks like she's done a lot of work while living in it, just like Carol and Larry are doing. The floor is wood now instead of dirt and she's built a greenhouse onto the kitchen, and in the greenhouse there's a big claw foot tub sitting right next to the tomato plants. There's a new stove and new cupboards with doors made out of thin red willows gathered from the creek. There's flowered cushions on the window sills to sit on and look across the fields, like at Carol's. It's turning to dusk now and I don't want to ask Mal for dinner, so I call Haud to come on and we go back through the fence to Claude's.

Claude is there at the kitchen table when we come in, looking over some papers by candlelight. He looks up at us and says, Howdy, and takes a long drag from his cigarette and goes back to looking at his papers. There are moths circling his head in the candlelight and dead ones all over the table from where they fly into the flame and get singed and croak. Croaked moths and cigarette butts and used wooden matches and coffee cups with gunk at the bottom cover the table. Wax has melted from the candle to a mound at its base, and there are more spent matches sticking up from the warm wax pile, which I fiddle with while asking Claude about maybe dinner or something to eat. I go over to the fridge but since there's no electricity it's empty and smells bad. There's nothing to eat, I think to myself and Haud complains out loud, and Claude says without looking up from his papers, Sure there is. There's bread and cheese. Make yourselves some cheese sandwiches. There's peanut butter too. I make two cheese sandwiches after first clearing a place on the counter, which is layered in dried dirty dishes and old newspapers and cast-iron pots with rusted liquid at the bottom. I paw through the magazines and find one to look at, a *New Yorker* with pictures of big fancy cars and women in fur coats. Then I find a sleeping bag wedged under the stairs and look for a place to sleep. There's no light in one of the rooms and I can't see in, so I put my bag on the floor in the other one where I can still get a little of the candle. I fall asleep listening to the hiss of Claude's cigarette and the pop of moths flying into the candle and a dog barking somewhere across the valley.

I wake up at first light and it's cold before the sun comes up. I'm stiff from sleeping on the cement floor. Stretching, shivering, rubbing one foot on the other to get it warm, I'm scratching a mosquito bite on my calf with one hand, and one on my top foot with the other hand. I'm wearing the clothes I slept in, and I pull a sweater out of my bag and it still smells like smoke from sitting by the campfires in California and I feel a painful tugging pressure in my chest, thinking about Ki. I pull the sweater on over my tangled hair and kick Haud to wake him up but he just mutters and rolls away from my foot. I wander into the kitchen and the dirt floor is cold and powdery.

There are still some crumbs on the counter from last night's sandwiches and there are even more cigarette butts. I walk out into the yard, stepping over some boxes of broken dishes and boards with nails in them and the caved-in windshield. I want to wash in the ditch but there's only a brown trickle, someone upstream must be irrigating today. I pee near the outhouse and then sit on a busted couch that I hadn't seen the night before, and I scratch myself and yawn and finally crawl back into my bag. I fall asleep again as the sun is hitting the tops of the cottonwoods along the creek, and wake up when Random comes over, dragging Kwikwi.

Chapter 17

Sears and Robot

Claude is never home. He drives off somewhere every day to do a job or something. I end up at Mal's mostly. She loves Random a lot and is a good mom to him, and I soak up the extra. She doesn't act like a mom to me but she's never mean, and she shows me how to do stuff and lets me bang away on her piano or use Random's paints and crayons. I help her weed the garden, the plants pulling easily up out of the moist dark soil. I help her pick and braid garlic and onions and string up bunches of dill and oregano and basil and mint, which she dries in the kitchen with cheesecloth under it to keep bits from dropping on the floor. We store potatoes and beets and carrots and apples in the root cellar, which is dark and cool and musty from the smell of years of storing fruit and vegetables. She drives her pickup truck to gather firewood, and me and Haud both come, gathering the rounds she cuts from public forest land and tossing them in the truck. Haud dances around her begging to use the chainsaw, and I peel pine pitch from my hands and roll it into little balls.

We throw hunks of wood into the truck until it's full and Mal drives us to Peñasco for popsicles from the general store. Peñasco is a little bigger than Dixon and in the opposite direction from Ojo Sarco. To get to Dixon you drive down the valley, and to get to Peñasco you drive up the valley. I also went to school in Peñasco for a while for first grade but the kids, all Chicano kids and no other white hippie kids, made too much fun of me. I used to wear a purple hat and an orange coat and a ballet tutu to school because they were my favorite clothes, but that was just too strange for all the kids in ironed dresses and belted shorts and pure white socks. But besides having a school Peñasco has a general store, and now food like popsicles is becoming important because there's never anything around to eat at Claude's.

Random and Haud and I hang around Mal's house together. Random sings to himself, drags the cat everywhere, and plays trucks with Haud. I swing in the hammock and make up games like school, where I'm the teacher and the schoolhouse is Mal's old not-too-dirty chicken coop. We try to teach Random how to ride the little bike Mal got for him, and we take turns zooming down the hill in his Green Machine and his Big Wheel. When Haud breaks the Green Machine and then the Big Wheel, both times by standing on the back when Random is driving, Mal yells at him, Go find your own damn toys. Claude needs to teach you kids some manners.

Banished from Mal's for a while, we pick through the junk in Claude's yard and house. There's crazy collections of stuff with no pattern or organization, just piles and boxes and bags everywhere.

In the yard among the weeds and apple trees going wild there are bags spilling old garbage no one's taken to the dump, boxes of wires and cables, tires and wheels, the rusting stove, broken dishes, big hunks of car or truck parts, boards, windows, tar paper. The New Mexico sun is at its hottest in the fall afternoons, and it's turned the yard and fields into arid burnt brown desert. Trees seem limp and dusty and weeds look like they might go up in flames. Looking at the yard, it feels like I'm in a trash desert, another place of lost and broken things.

The house is cooler but just as dirty and broken. There are four rooms, the kitchen and a front room next to it that has a cement floor, a room behind the kitchen with a dirt floor that could be a bedroom or a living room but for some reason has holes dug all over the floor so you can't use it, and next to that a room that Claude uses like workshop. There's also an attic. The kitchen has the woodstove and the broken fridge and the wire-spool table and the drunk chair with flaking-off green paint. There's a sink, it has running water. The front room has a cement floor and a metal frame couch with plastic cushions leaking foam rubber stuffing. At one end of the front room is a tiny winding stair case that leads up to the attic.

The attic stairs are so narrow and steep they're like a ladder. At the top of this ladder is one long room, part of it a wood floor and part of it just humps of dirt that used to be the roof before there was an attic, I guess. On the humps of dirt there are heaps of old clothes and cartons of books. On the wood part there are two sleeping bags for me and Haud, with a sheet hung between them. There's an old piece of rug, and in a corner is a tin can that I found, when I cautiously smelled it, was full of old pee and dead flies, and which I haven't emptied because it's too gross and because I might spill it going down the stairs, so it just sits there drowning more flies. There's also a broken dresser spilling more old clothes.

With nothing to do and no way of measuring time, I lose track of these long dry days, one after the other the same, just me and Haud rummaging through stuff, like wild coyotes looking for food. In the yard Haud looks for parts to small motors, and with a pan of gasoline and a toothbrush he cleans the parts like he's seen Claude and Larry do. He looks for wires and small batteries and cogs and gears and tiny wheels, and he makes weird little things, bending over some scattered newspapers stained with oil and gas with his butt hanging out of his jeans and his hair hanging in his eyes. Like Claude and like Larry and like any man I have ever watched build things or take things apart, he curses and swears and mutters under his breath, saying, This fucker's on too tight , or Just a cunt hair more, or Come on you bitch. I look for stuff, I don't know what kind of stuff, just stuff. I find an old aspirin tin and a pearl-handled pocket knife with a broken blade and the clasp of an old bracelet.

In the attic I pull through the piles and boxes of clothes looking for something to wear, but it's all army coats stiff with age, or tee shirts worn thin and full of holes from moths or battery acid or mismatched socks or greasy jeans. I take all of the boxes of books apart and they're all grownup books and I end up reading them anyway, even though I don't understand most of them. There's Steven King, about a town full of vampires, which I love. There's Marquis de Sade about fucking and there's *Animal Farm* about a farm of animals that talk and think and fight with each other about who's in control. There's *The Lord of the Flies* about kids stranded on an island, which I also love. There's medical textbooks full of pictures of lesions and wounds. There's *Catcher in the Rye, Brave New World,* and *1984.* It doesn't matter what it's about, I read them all, sitting hunched in the hot attic for hours until I'm cramped stiff and sore and finally have to go downstairs and look for something to eat or go pee in the yard. It's too much trouble to go all the way to the outhouse, and besides, it stinks really bad in the heat.

In Claude's workshop are the things that save me. In more swollen cartons of auto repair manuals Haud finds a catalog and gives it to me, Here, I found a Sears and Robot, you can have it. There's also a bunch of seed catalogs. In the still afternoons with nothing moving but cicadas I look through the catalogs, going over each page slowly.

The Sears catalog is my favorite. There's everything you could want, pages and pages, all in shiny colors. Clothes and jewelry and beds and rocking chairs and matching washcloths and towels. Plates with lilac patterns on them and yellow curtains made of dotted swiss and pink princess canopies for girls' rooms. I forget everything around me and make up a whole world where all the furniture matches and I have all the clothes I want. Filmy green dresses with pink bow sashes, little white sandals with daisies on them, beaded purses, frilly bathing suits with matching swimming caps. I plan whole rooms with pink and white wicker furniture and beds covered in quilts that have strawberries all over them and look like huge pieces of cake.

When I'm worn out with wanting these things I look through the seed catalogs, bright beautiful pictures of peach trees in bloom and baskets of peaches, rose-covered arbors, fields of daffodils, wheelbarrows overflowing with ripe tomatoes and crisp cucumbers and swollen lettuce heads and carrots so orange they look like candy. On pieces of graph paper that I find in Claude's workshop I draw miniature gardens, carefully planning where the zinnias, the hollyhocks, the pansies, the gazebo, and the raspberries go. I plan the vegetable garden, neat rows of radishes and peas and watermelons. I spend days and days doing this. In the evenings by candlelight, when Claude is home and poring over his auto manuals, I cut pictures out of the catalogs and glue them up, putting clumps of plums and apples and apricots on the doorjambs and fields of poppies and irises on the walls.

On a day when Claude is home I ask him can we order some stuff from the seed catalog. He says planting season is over but I'll see what I can do. When he comes home next he hands me a packet of zinnia seeds, saying These are hardy. He is perched up high in the cab of the dump truck, handing the seeds down to me through the open door. I'm clinging to the door frame, my toes gripping the hot metal of the running board, asking him about tomatoes and lettuce too. Claude is fiddling with something on the dashboard, the choke maybe, looking out over the steering wheel but not seeing anything, I can tell, he's got a look of intense concentration on his face while he listens to the engine. He smells like sweat and smoke and adobe and he says quiet down, I need to hear this, and he gives me a little shove off the truck.

Out in the front of the yard underneath the kitchen window I take a hoe and the packet of seeds and I spend the afternoon trying to turn the baked hard earth into a bed for the zinnias. In my bare feet I hop up and down on the shovel to break the earth and I stop when the soles of my feet hurt too much and I have dizzy spots from working in the sun with no breakfast because I was too excited about planting my zinnias to make a cheese sandwich or open a can of sardines. Finally the earth is loose enough for me to rake it and I scatter the seeds and carefully cover them. I water them with a watering can made out of a coffee can that Haud poked full of holes for me. Every day I look for the seeds to come up and they do but they dry up quickly in the sun. Anyway I forget to water them because now I have another project, which is raking years of chicken shit out of the old coop in the orchard to make a school or a playhouse.

The chicken coop sits in a tangle of mustard weeds and ragweed and has a little screen door and a little window and if it weren't so full of grey-white chicken droppings and feathers it would make the perfect little house. Using a hoe and a shovel I pry at the droppings, sneezing, covered in shit dust and cobwebs, scratching myself on the rusted screens and nails poking out everywhere. I give up when I get too spooked by the spiders and too discouraged by the amount of chicken shit still stuck everywhere. For a while I just sit under one of the gnarled apple trees, looking at the coop and making it nice in my mind. I drag the catalog over, and in my mind I put up curtains and there's rugs and a flower box on the windowsill. Me and Ki live there and I plan all the furniture, the little space becoming much bigger in my mind. I plant a garden outside of it and Ki and I have birthday parties in matching flowered dresses and we go to school in our matching capes and shoes with little bows on them.

I fall asleep under the tree, drooling on the catalog. I wake up, hot and limp in the sun, nostrils caked in powdered droppings, when a car goes by with a bunch of Chicano boys in it, whooping and throwing beers cans out of the window. I look around at the junk in the yard, and it looks like a war started here, a war that left everything broken and desolate and jagged. Oil- and gasoline-soaked rags hang limply from tree branches, car seats leak their guts, nails poke out from everything, grass and weeds are dead and greasy where gas and oil has spilled on them.

In the cool dimness of the kitchen I get myself water from the sink, drinking out of a Mason jar. The counter is made of scrap plywood and doesn't have drawers or doors on the cupboard. The cupboards hold faded mismatched plastic dishes and odd things like a colander missing two legs, and the blades but not the motor of an electric mixer, and half a blender. I sit at the spool table and listen for the sound of Claude's truck coming back.

Chapter 18

I Can't Get Enough of You Baby

Me and Random and Josie, who's three or four and lives down the road, are at the creek below our houses. The creek runs through the lowest part of the valley, and all along it there are willows and cottonwoods and in some places small pools and marshes. It runs shallow and it's cold because it comes down from the snowmelt in the mountains, and it's full of interesting weeds, watercress, mint, horsetails, Queen Anne's lace. There's no place big enough to swim exactly but there's places you can lie down and get your head underwater. We wade through it looking for snakes. It's shady and dimly green beneath the willows, and the beds of watercress have small white flowers. We sit on a tree that fell across the creek long ago, our legs dangling down, not quite touching the water. The tree is worn smooth from feet running across it, my toes know the way without even checking.

At the other side of the creek is a well, just a square lip of boards to tell where it is, so old it's grown over with tree roots and the boards are falling in. We lie on our stomachs and try to see it. I heard Mal talking the other day about how Aaron's little brother Shoshone fell into the creek and drowned and how now his mom is crazy. Would anyone miss me if I fell into the well? How long would it be before anyone noticed I was gone? For sure no one would notice in time to save me. Two or three days, I guess to myself. After careful thought I decide it would be a longer time than that. Claude would just assume I was at Mal's and Mal would just assume I was at Claude's. There are days when I don't see Claude at all. I wake up in the middle of the night knowing the house is empty. At first I would wander around the house looking for him, aching and confused. Where were you? I accused him the next time I saw him, and he said, I left a candle burning with a note by it. Didn't you see it? No.

After the creek we walk up the other side of the field, where there is an old corral that used to have horses and an old barn. The floor is covered in straw and horse shit and there are bits of old leather stuff hanging on the walls, harnesses and reins and bits and rusted horseshoes. Light seeps in through the cracks in the boards and makes horizontal planes of dust motes, swirly magical windows flowering tiny planets that revolve in the still air. Someone is coming up the path from the creek. Todd and Becky, Josie's older brother and sister.

Josie is round and blond and looks like Shirley Temple, all dimples and snubby nose. Becky, who's in her teens, looks like a dark-haired version of Shirley Temple. Todd, the oldest, maybe fifteen or sixteen, looks like a boy Shirley Temple with the beginnings of a faint feathery mustache and beard. Peeking out of the cracks in the wall, I watch them walk up, arguing softly. Becky has boobs bouncing around under her pink shirt. Todd is wiry with muscle and I have a pretty bad crush on him, ever since

I was six. As they walk in the barn, squinting in the change of light, he says, Hey sweetie heart to Josie and Hey sour fart to me.

They have cigarettes to smoke here in the barn. I fiddle with my shirt, which is wet and muddy from the creek and has burrs stuck all in it from the walk up through the field. I'm sure I have burrs in my hair too, and my shoulders hunch in on themselves in embarrassment like I'm trying to hide in my own skin. Becky looks at me like I'm a turd. I'm twelve but I might as well be five for all the attention she pays me. Even though I've known Todd and Becky and Josie for years, we're not friends because I don't really live here. It's like that with all the kids around here, Aaron and Brad and Kiva that live in Canoncito, Michael Brown who lives farther down the valley almost in Dixon, Magpie and Podgie who at one time lived near Mal's. I used to play Barbies with Magpie and Podgie, and their dad once brought a Christmas tree home one night and in the morning the tree was all covered in ribbons and had presents under it. Who did that? I wanted to know, Santa Claus, their dad said, and for a little while I almost believed him. We made our Barbies hump and watched the cat giving birth to kittens in the attic. I saw Magpie and Podgie in Canoncito a little while ago and all they said was, We're not called that anymore, looking at me the same way Becky is now. Our names are Pamela and Pauline. The other day Haud peed in an apple juice bottle and tried to get Josie to drink it.

Todd is leaning against the barn wall, holding a cigarette like my dad does, between his first two fingers. He is eyeing me through half-closed eyes, the smoke swirling in the horizontal beams of light. The downy fuzz on his cheeks catches glints of sun. So what's California like? he asks lazily, and I shrug. Did you go to the beach a lot? Were there surfer chicks in bikinis? I want to fix up this old jeep and drive around the boardwalk in Santa Cruz, he says, inhaling deeply like he's toking on a joint. Santa Cruz is bitchin', he nods knowingly. I'm trying to think up an interesting lie to make up about surfer chicks in bikinis. Becky is sitting on a bale of hay and she says, Don't bogart, Todd, you're such a hog. Now you're the sour fart and Clane's my sweetie heart, Todd says, handing the cigarette to Becky. She inhales and coughs. Josie and Random are quiet, just watching. I hug my shoulders, trying to make myself less visible. Todd says suddenly, Hey Becky, I know that one guy likes you, the one who sits on the back of the bus with me, you know, Tommy. You going to make out with him? Todd turns to face the wall and wraps his arms around himself so just his hands show, which he slides up and down his own back going mmmmm kiss me you fool, and me and the kids are busting out laughing. Now Becky will just hate me more. She's looking at me like go ahead and laugh, I'll get you later.

Todd sits down on the bale next to Becky and picks at the calluses on his hands and says I'm bored, let's drive up to Peñasco and try to score some beer. They leave. I walk back up to

Claude's and the kids tag after me but I'm mean to them and they go off together, looking for Haud.

Haud is rummaging through boxes in Claude's workshop, wild-haired and scabby, brown with dirt. I sit on the broken sofa in the front room, stupid with heat and boredom. I listen to the sound of cicadas on the juniper bushes on the ridge and then fall asleep in another hot silence, foam-rubber crumbs sticking to my shirt and shorts. I wake up with drool on my arm, heavy and confused with sleep. Todd is outside with a Chicano boy, one of the boys that drive down the road fast, throwing beer cans. They're looking for Claude to help them with one of the cars they're fixing up but I don't know where Claude is and I sit on the plastic couch, the imprint of the plastic on my face, blinking and trying to get the taste of greasy sleep out of my mouth. The boys sits on a pile of boards outside, smoking, waiting for Claude. I hang in the doorway for a minute, not knowing what to do, rubbing one crusty foot on top of the other. Todd asks me have you heard of this one band, Kiss? No. He sings, I was made for loving you baby, were you made for loving me? I can't get enough of you baby, can you get enough of me?

Chapter 19

Now Is a Place, Huge but Empty

First my uncle Matt comes with his girlfriend, Debbie, and then my uncle Chris comes too, all from Nevada. Matt is the younger of my two uncles and has blond hair and a wide grinning face. He came in a Toyota, pretty new, with a motorcycle in the back and Debbie sitting next to him in the truck. His truck with the motorcycle in it is parked in the yard and Haud is hanging over the tailgate of the truck, looking at the motorcycle with pure love in his eyes. Claude and Matt are standing near the truck drinking beers and talking about motors and about Matt's drive to New Mexico from Las Vegas and about Claude's backhoe. I'm hanging on the tire swing watching Debbie, who is young and pretty with long blonde hair.

Debbie wears a halter dress with flowers on it and sits on a stump holding a beer, her legs crossed, her sandals brushing over the wood chips. She holds the can of Hamm's delicately with her pinkie raised, and she smokes a cigarette, taking huge drags while the men lean on the truck and say things about horsepower and two-stroke engines and cams.

They brought groceries and Debbie makes sloppy joes on the woodstove and offers us some, and Claude grumbles, I don't want you kids eating that junk, and Haud and I stare at him openmouthed, like cans of sardines aren't junk? Matt mops his plate of sloppy joes with white bread, and Debbie eats as delicately as she drinks.

Mostly we have been foraging for our own food, making sandwiches and eating granola from the box between sips of evaporated milk from the can, or saltines gobbed with jelly. Sometimes we hang around Mal's until she gives in and feeds us, sometimes Claude will come home with a bag of groceries and light a fire in the stove and say to me, Go wash some dishes in the ditch and to Haud, Go on over to Mal's and borrow some chard or kale. Then he'll fry an onion and bacon together in the heavy cast-iron pan and put groats in it and then kale and eggs over that and we'll say, What's for dinner and he'll say, Stuff. What are you making? Stuff. Stuff's not so bad, melted cheese on top. I'd rather have sloppy joes, though.

Matt and Debbie move into a small lean-to down by the creek. It has a little stove in it and a bench covered in blankets that they use as a bed. I spend a lot of time there. Debbie is pretty and funny and sweet, she says, Come here you little ragamuffin and I stand between her legs with my back to her while she combs the tangles out of my hair and fixes my shell necklace and ties it back on for me. You haven't washed your neck all summer, have you? she says, holding my hair up, and she gives me soap to use in the ditch. She gives me Spam between slices of white bread smeared with sandwich spread and handfuls of Fritos and sips of her beer. Matt and Debbie sit on a board over two rocks in front of the lean-to and they smoke pot and we listen to the creek and watch for fireflies.

The broken-down house and the trashed yard have been feeling to me like I'm caught in a no-man's-land, a place where time doesn't pass. Like time forgets me. Like I just woke up from sleep to find myself here in this place, with no idea of how or why. I wouldn't know how to say this if anyone asked me. The world is made up of places but I live somewhere between places. This is a feeling I get when I'm standing in a field getting a pricker out of my foot or when I wake up in the hot afternoon on the couch in the front room or when I look up from a book in the attic. I can see myself from above, this is me and this is a place and I used to understand the movement from one place to another but am starting not to. What is going to happen next is a question I never ask. Now is a thing which feels huge but empty. This feeling goes away a little when Matt and Debbie come.

Debbie comes up to the house to wash her hair in the sink, bent over the counter with the back of her neck showing white and covered in flowery-smelling lather. The water only runs cold but not too cold to stand, and she says, Come here I'll wash yours too. She wraps her hair in a clean towel and tucks it into a turban and stands me on a milk crate next to the sink. With her fingers rubbing my scalp I realize it's been maybe months since anyone touched me, since a woman's hands have smoothed my hair or rubbed my shoulders. She puts conditioner in my hair too, also smelling like flowers, and she wraps my head up like hers and we sit on the stoop. Debbie smokes a cigarette and says, This place is a rat hole. Claude really ought to fix this place up. What are all those holes doing in your floor? Instead of feeling embarrassed for Claude and defending him I agree with her and we say men are pigs, just pigs, and she snorts and we giggle.

Matt comes in with greasy hands from working on his motorcycle and says, What are you ladies scheming up now? I like Matt. He growls his words and pops beer cans open loudly and reads to us from the books he reads, which are always about people either fighting or fucking. People fucking embarrasses me, but Matt gives the characters funny voices and then after a bit he will clap the book shut and say, You kids shouldn't be hearing this.

When uncle Chris comes he brings a truck too and also a motorcycle, and now the yard is full of trucks and bikes and men talking motors. They lean over the hoods and peer at the undercarriages and say, The mix is too rich you need to adjust the carburetor, and That knock sounds like a timing problem and they say, It's the gap on the spark plugs. They use words like *manifold* and *compressor* and *gasket*. Chris has a honking big nose and has dishwater-brown hair that is a little long and curly. He also has only three fingers on one hand from where he blew one finger off with firecrackers, and he makes that hand into an alien claw for us. Only once or twice though, he doesn't joke like Matt does.

Chris and Claude huddle together over batteries, over tires, over radiators. Claude is lean and dusty and burned brown except where his shirt stops at the back of his neck and his arms. He has a bristly mustache and beard and his eyes are always fixed on something I can't see, peering at an engine or over books or magazines or squinting across the field talking about something he's going to build. Haud scoots from one open hood to another hopping up on the bumpers to stand tippy-toes to look at running engines and Claude or Chris or Matt will say, Keep your paws outta there Haudie. Chris will cuff him, not hard, and say, Go do something useful.

Chris is taller than Matt and Matt is taller than Claude. Claude is the oldest, then Chris, then Matt. They don't look alike, you wouldn't know they were brothers. Chris wears glasses like Claude, and I notice that like Claude he is thin and lean with ropy muscles and permanently work-scarred hands, always with gunk under their nails, always deep creases worn in the tips of their fingers.

Todd comes over too and all the men drink beer and smoke joints and argue about engines or cars or motorcycles. They draw each other diagrams and jab the air with their fingers and Claude says, Well what you're talking about is horsepower and Chris says, What I'm talking about is efficiency. Claude says, She'll still do ninety in third and Matt says, Yeah but you have to work on that piece of shit every day.

The men work on their cars and Debbie watches, stoned, and Haud hangs on every word and Random sucks his thumb and twirls handfuls of hair, eyes wide around the grubby fat fist in his mouth. I sit on a stump nearby, holding the Sears catalog. The pages are curling up and it's lost its cover. I look at yellow bedspreads covered in daisies and fluffy round rugs and vanity tables wearing ruffled skirts. I look at pillow shams covered in satin ribbons. The men go to Peñasco for more Coors and Hamm's and they carefully roll cigarettes out of blue Bugler cans, swaying a little, as the sun dips below the ridge and shadows fall across the valley and the night air gets cooler.

Chapter 20
Cicada and Juniper

Claude is majordomo of the irrigation-ditch committee. I
don't know what a majordomo is, but the irrigation-ditch
committee gets together sometimes to drink beer and worry
about the dry weather and talk about who's hogging the ditch
water. They also collect dues. A sack of ten-dollar rolls of
quarters sits in the kitchen just begging me and Haud to take a
roll, which we do. The men are up on the ridge riding the
motorcycles they fixed and Debbie is in the lean-to by the creek,
listening to a transistor radio, painting her toenails, stoned.

With a roll of quarters, me and Haud walk the two or
three miles up the road to the post office, ambling in the heat,
pausing to walk more slowly and go, Hey there, hey there it's
okay, when the mean dogs come out to the road. German
shepherds, brindle bulldogs, and border collies with matted ruffs
come to stand in the driveways, bristling and ferocious. We edge
around them, walking sideways to the other side of the road. We
keep to the sparse patches of shade made by the cottonwoods and
we stop and watch when a truck or a car goes by us. We pass a
few young kids hanging around porches, dark-haired silent
Chicano boys who go still when they see us and watch us pass. We
go by an old man rocking on his porch, smoking, and we go by

another old man standing by an outhouse, slowly buckling his belt over his jeans.

At the post office we spend the roll of quarters on sodas and candy. Pepsi, Three Musketeers, barbecue potato chips. Huge wads of Bazooka Joe and Tootsie Pops, grape for Haud and cherry for me. We're tired and stuffed but there's nothing to do but walk back the same way we came.

Halfway back we're dying of thirst even after the sodas. Haud says, Hecacita sells milk, maybe we can buy some. We have two dollars left. We take a few steps down the long driveway to her house and we stop while the dogs bark at us. Halted by the barking, pacing dogs, we wait for one of her sons or daughters to come. A young man comes, wearing a John Deere baseball cap and blue jeans ironed stiff and cowboys boots, and he jerks the dogs by their collars.

Hecacita's house is just like Mamacita's, spackled gray and white, low to the ground, with a cement porch and a tin roof. It has a dirt floor and the same faded wallpaper and Formica table worn white in four places in front of the chairs, which are carefully patched with duct tape. Her daughter Dorothy is there. Hecacita and Dorothy are standing in the dim cool kitchen, stirring beans.

Dorothy has a round fat face and two long black tight braids, and I would say her face is genial but she is one of the girls who stole my purple hat with the blue ribbon when I went to first grade in Peñasco. I don't know if she recognizes me or remembers this but I do. Dorothy always wears jeans and a jean jacket and they always look brand new, with a checked shirt under the jacket. Her body is solid and thick and it was this way even when we were six, and it surprises me that I suddenly remember this much about her, that seeing her in her mother's kitchen on this hot day when I am twelve feels just like I am six again. Dorothy is another thing that has stayed still and in the same place while I have been other places, another landmark like the slanting barn. I seat myself carefully at the table, solemn and deliberate in this clean kitchen.

Hecacita moves slow like her bones are creaking. Haud waits by the fridge while she moves gallon jars of milk around. She gives him one and I give her the two dollars and we are going to carry the milk home, taking turns because it's so heavy, but Hecacita's son has brought a rusted red wagon onto the porch for us to use. I feel guilty, somehow, about this piece of niceness. A red wagon, and we put the milk in it and walk slowly up the driveway. Back on the road we open the milk and take long drinks from the heavy, slickly cold jar, wiping white trails from our faces and getting it on our shirts. It's a little sour. Hecacita gave us sour milk but probably not on purpose. We drink anyway and walk home pulling the wagon.

Chapter 21

Hey, Where you Going?

My family of men is dusty and greasy with motor oil and smells like gasoline and beer and sweat and tobacco. Chris stands in the yard looking thoughtfully up at the eaves of the roof, where there is a bunch of wires sticking out from when the house had electricity. Reading or playing cards by candlelight, Chris says, You should really think about getting some electric in here. Matt looks up from his latest book, *Venus on the Half-Shell*, and says, Yeah you're living in the Dark Ages here. Dark ages, heh-heh, get it, he says, winking at me. Claude, annoyed, harrumphs loudly and throws his book down and says, We're fine here without electricity. Chris jerks his head at me, standing in the doorway with my sleeping bag draped over my shoulders, holding my tattered catalog, and Haud curled up asleep on the broken couch covered in one of Claude's coats, and says, Sure, Claude. You're fine. The kids look fine. The air is thick with arguments. Claude snorts and goes out to the shitter.

When the men are all home Matt fiddles with a huge tape machine that he brought with him from Las Vegas. He spent all of one day hooking weird things up to other weird things, the tape machine, which is a reel-to-reel, and a car battery and cables and bits of wire and duct tape. Lookit that, he says, downing a beer with a burp and patting the machine. We've got music now. The reel-to-reel hums and then with a whup whup whup the tape catches and we're listening to Led Zeppelin for a few minutes before the machine winds to a halt.

Claude and Chris play Go. Using a carpenter's pencil Claude traces an even grid of squares on a piece of plywood and they use this as their game board. There are Go boards all over the house, and empty beer cans, and cans of Bugler. Go is a three-thousand-year-old game of war strategy, Claude says, rolling a Bugler cigarette, leaning back in a chair, the legs tilted way off the ground. I sit nearby reading *Fear and Loathing in Las Vegas*. That's where we're going, Matt says, hooking a thumb at the book. Where? I ask. Las Vegas, he says. Where your grandma is. He messes with the tape machine some more and then thumps his fists onto his thighs in tune with the music. Way way down inside, you neeeeed me, the tape machine sings, before dying again.

When no one is home I wander around looking for someone, for Claude mostly. When I can't find him I say again and again, Where were you? Where were you? I was across the valley, he answers. Didn't you see the truck? I honked the horn and I called but you didn't hear, so I went to Española without you. Thought you didn't want to come. The inside of me feels like a tin can in a huge crusher being squeezed tighter and tighter under heavy pressure. Slow you blow, snooze you lose. I will always be left behind or alone, will always miss the thing that's happening, be late or in the wrong place. The deep unfairness of this.

I don't know when it was decided that me and Haud were going to Las Vegas. I never heard anyone talking about it. Claude doesn't say anything about it when he is around, which lately is never. When he is around there is a thick feeling to the air and a lot of arguments between him and Matt and Chris. During these arguments, which seem to be about nothing or anything, Matt stares at the counter or the wall or out the window and fiddles with things, while Chris folds his arms carefully and looks at his feet, and Claude gets puffy like a rooster and talks loudly, moving his hands in the air and jabbing at things as he makes some point about four-wheel drive or whether Honda is better than Harvester International or what time of the season the roads get bad. Electricity jumps between them, jumping off Claude the strongest, his voice the loudest, always having the last word. Just before the argument becomes a fight one of the uncles gives in, usually Chris. Matt just says things under his breath.

Over at Mal's the garden has been harvested and she is busy teaching Random piano and mudding the house for winter. She sniffs when I say we're going to Las Vegas and she doesn't say anything but makes a small sound in the back of her throat. I ask her about Lore but I get the feeling she doesn't like Lore. I don't remember anything about Lore. I don't even remember when it was that I knew I had uncles, much less another grandmother.

While the days are still hot the night gets cold, cold enough to make the aspens change color and the cottonwoods start to lose some of their leaves, which blow around in a fitful wind. A milky hot sun seeps through the leaves left on the trees, turning them bright gold, and I watch them from the front room, the lilac bushes now brown and the gooseberry bushes red.

On another afternoon when I am in the attic reading *Still Life with Woodpecker* I hear a truck pulling up, a truck with a knock to it, Todd's truck. I know it's the valves, that knock, I have hung in the doorway of Claude's shop listening to Chris and Claude saying, It's the valves, she's going to throw a rod, listen to that knock, gun it for a sec, Todd. The truck spits gravel down the drive and Todd honks the horn. Also sitting in the front seat is Mercy and a boy. Mercy is wearing a white blouse, bright white against the cracked vinyl of the seat, she's in the middle between the two boys. I hang in the doorway like always, with my scaly feet and cutoffs, and I tell Todd that Chris is in Peñasco getting parts and that Matt is down at the creek and I don't know where Claude is. They sit in the truck and the engine creaks. Todd says, We were hoping someone has a little weed and I shrug. We're going to a party, want to come? Get in the back, little guys in the back. I don't want to be a little guy and I don't want to be in the back of the truck all the way down the valley, going to a party where all the Chicano girls like Mercy will have neat ironed clothes and combed hair and all the Ojo Sarco and Dixon boys will sit in their trucks laughing big at nothing and arguing about who goes on a beer run next. I melt back into the house. Todd guns the truck backwards up the driveway and I hear them rattling and knocking down the road.

No one is around for what seems like all day. I go over to Mal's and she's asleep with a book over her face. Random and Haud must be over at Josie's. I set off along the road and stop at Josie's, calling from the top of the drive, but no one answers. I go around the bend and haul myself, tired and dispirited, up the hill where the church is, thinking I'll go by Carol and Larry's, maybe Claude will be there. I pass clumps of milkweed growing by the side of the road, the pods beginning to burst open, and I snap off a stem to watch the bitter white milk form. I pass the apple trees with their gnarled branches and small hard fruit. Those apples are as hard as a twelve-year-old's tits, I once heard Todd say, and I looked down at my chest, flat as a boy's. I pass the melting hole in the ground where the school was going to be.

A long purple car, low to the ground, comes around the bend and slows to a stop where I am, pressed into some juniper bushes, hoping no one sees me. Mariachi music comes loud from the radio. There are two Chicano boys in front and one in back. Someone turns the music down and the car idles loudly, shaking. I look at the boys, not saying anything. Hey where you going? the one who's driving asks, in the soft singsong way that Chicanos in New Mexico speak English. Looking for my father, I say, one foot inching its way up onto the other foot, hands deep in my pockets, shoulders hunched all the way up to my ears. Who's your father?

Claude, I say. You want a ride? We'll go around the valley, help you look.

The boy in the back opens the door and slides over to give me room. The darkness of the interior is like a mouth but the boys are quiet, waiting, and I climb in. My feet don't reach the floor of the car and I sit against the door and stare at a spot below the driver's head. He turns the music back up but not too loud. We drive slowly around the whole valley and the boys don't say anything except once to ask, Is that your father? but it's not, it's Jim Stahl, who maybe looks a little like my father. The boys are maybe fifteen or sixteen. I can get out here, I say just before Claude's house, and the car stops, rumbling, and I pick my way down the gravel of the drive.

Matt and Chris are home. Where ya been? one asks, deep in an engine. Looking for you all, I accuse, near tears. We got the electric turned on, Chris says proudly. The tape machine is blaring Herbie Hancock in the workshop and there is a floodlight strung from the ceiling and even the empty fridge is humming. I am tired, really really tired. I can look at my catalog by electric light now but the light just makes everything look dirtier, the floor with huge holes dug in it, the cracking plaster, the unfinished wooden cupboards turned grimy black from hands opening the drawers without handles, the boxes of junk, piles of cigarette butts, stacks of books about fucking, my sour dirty sleeping bag crumpled in a corner.

Chapter 22

Here You Go, Sugar

We left Ojo Sarco behind, me and Haud in the front of Matt's truck, Matt driving cheerfully and carelessly, whistling, all our belonging tied down under a tarp in the back. Just our clothes, really. Matt said, Don't even bother bringing that sleeping bag with you, Lore won't even let you in the house with it. Yeah, she'll chase it out with a broom, Chris had laughed. And don't bother bringing those books, Clanie, she's got every book you could ever want. Matt's toolboxes are tucked into the back, too. A big truck, I had to hang onto the door with one hand and use the other to haul myself up into the cab.

First we bumped up the valley toward the highway, the crunch of the fat tires on gravel, Matt driving fast and lifting two fingers off the wheel to passing cars and trucks, Lawrence Sandoval, Pedro Leyba's son, Martin Espinosa. We passed Dorothy working over the chopping block in Hecacita's yard, her braids swinging. Past the post office and no more grape Nehi for a very long time and the next time I did drink it it didn't taste the same. Haud in the middle of the seat and me at the window, hanging out the window and watching the valley recede behind us as we turned onto the highway and built up speed for the big hill before the horseshoe bend in the road, then into Truchas. A right turn at Truchas, a town that sits on top of a high ridge, just a few adobe buildings squatting low to the ground facing mesas that go on for miles, the mesas disappearing into the grey-blue haze of juniper-covered mountains. The road dips down the valley around sandstone hills. Matt took the curves fast and lazy, one hand draped over the steering wheel, the other across the back of the seat, blue eyes squinted almost shut against the sun. The wind whipped past my face, smelling of sage and juniper and cool mountain air.

I watched the road for a long time, through Santa Fe and into Albuquerque, and then I slept, curled into Matt's jacket, my face pressed against the window. Haud nodded beside me, his face dropping to his chest, his matted hair in his eyes. I woke up to the high whistling roar of trucks going fast beside us, the rush of huge tires and creaking trailers, slept again, woke again to the thump and bump of the tires going over a driveway to stop beside some gas pumps. I smelled gas and exhaust as I went looking for a bathroom, hoisted myself heavy-lidded up onto the toilet. I woke again to country music, Matt changing the radio station, going from Waylon and Willie and the boys to Maria Muldar, "Midnight at the Oasis," to Phoebe Snow, to Led Zeppelin, where Matt let the dial rest. Woke up again to Matt cursing, the truck swerving off the road, the smell of smoke. A cigarette butt landing in the back of the truck had set something on fire. I worried about this for the rest of the trip, what if a spark was still lit, what if it was next to a gas can, what if we blew up.

We drove out of New Mexico at the southeastern tip of the state and I watched a blank pane of nothing for a while. A few tall cactus plants, tumbleweeds gathered at the edges of fences, dry arroyos winding through tin culverts. Danger Flash Floods, signs said. Gusty Winds May Be Present. I liked being in the truck with Matt, maybe because he growled and joked, sang along with the radio, was present in a way Claude would not be. Claude's eyes are always seeing something beyond the horizon that is invisible to me, listening to something I can't hear, but Matt's eyes are always glinting and flashing. He howled along with the radio, I'm a smoker, I'm a joker, midnight toker, get my lovin on the run. He poked Haud in the ribs and said, Love 'em and leave 'em, hey Haudie? I could be near Matt and feel the solidity of who he was, a man who laughed at jokes along with us like he was a kid himself.

The small space of the cab kept me closed in from the flat nothing of the desert as it became even more dry and sparse, no towns, not even any road signs for a long time. The truck vibrated over the black ribbon of the highway, and the highway seemed like something patient and tough living alone under a huge sky.

The movement of the truck lulled me back into sleep, especially as we drove into night. As we got closer to Nevada, a place I had never seen, I dreamt of Ki, lost in vast white plains and dark jungles, crying for me. I ran from window to window in a pale city, creeping out onto ledges high above the bleached streets, looking for some landmark or direction, thinking I had to get to Ki, had to save her, she was lost somewhere in the echoing din of the whitewashed maze. I crept along an endless twining of paths worn into the jungle floor, my feet swimming in stinking, sucking blackness. Twists of vines hung in my face, dark fronds that kept me from seeing where I was going. Flowers I had never seen before, with old gnarled faces and hands that stretched at my ankles, lined the path crying with ugliness and fear. Ki was lost and I would never get to her. Choked and desperate to find my sister, I woke up crying, my insides one hollow well of keening lostness and loneliness. Not wanting Matt to see me crying, I huddled deeper into his jacket and tried to keep my shoulders from shaking. Quietly snuffling the wetness from my nose and face, I said, I miss my sister, Matt. I thought he didn't hear me but then he said, Where is she? I don't know, I said. She's with Helene. Where's Helene? I don't know, California? He said something between a growl and a cough, uncomfortable with having a crying twelve-year old girl in his truck, I'm sure she's fine. Knowing he was uncomfortable shut me up and put a layer over me that helped me hold my feelings in, and I quieted myself down and pressed my hot face onto the window pane and burrowed deeper into the coat.

The thought of Ki's face turned up to watch me leaving on the bus was more than I could bear, a loss as big as the sky I was traveling under, a feeling as emptied-out as the high droning whistle of the wind going past outside. I slept again and woke to a tuneless noise of no station on the radio that reminded me of the water tower on the abandoned ranch. With the high lonesome no-song playing at the edge of my waking mind I saw again the rolling waves of grass going off into forever and felt the endless hopeless patience of waiting for something that would never come.

We stopped to eat at diners sitting in the middle of vast acres of parking lots, surrounded by the rumbling of big rigs idling. We ran to stretch out our aching muscles and then sat at red vinyl booths swinging our legs while thin wizened waitresses with big hair put plastic glasses of soda on the tables in front of us and we didn't even have to ask. There were miniature jukeboxes at each table and Matt gave us nickels to play music. Stand by your man, give him all the love you can. In dreams, I walk, with you. We ate skinny hard french fries and grilled cheese sandwiches and pie.

Those diners where we ate were full of flies and men with sideburns wearing big dark glasses. They sat hunched over cups of coffee alone at the counters, their big knees splayed out to the side of their stools, or they sat in groups in the booths, leaning low over the table to speak to each other in voices I couldn't hear, but I could hear the tone their voices made. Low drawls and then cackles of laughter, someone slapping their knee or the top of the table. The coffee cups bounced and the waitress would come around with the pot again going, How 'bout a warm-up, here you go, sugar. I felt small around these men but not in a bad way, they opened doors for me and Haud to go first ahead of them with their big-knuckled hands. They might look over at us from time to time while we ate, with neither curiosity nor disinterest, nothing burning in their gaze.

We were almost there now, Matt said, and he drove different, both hands on the wheel, maybe eagerness to get there, and I felt a squiggle of excitement in my belly too. What's Lore like, we wanted to know, me and Haud, and Matt said, Her bark's worse than her bite. What's her house like, we asked. It's big, Matt growled, big enough for the two of you to get lost in. You kids just mind your manners and stay out of her way. She's going to take care of you for Claude.

We're going to go over the Hoover dam now, Matt said, and slowed down to let us look. A huge wall of water crashed from the holes in the dam down to the turbines churning below, turning the base of the dam into a thundering white roar. It was bigger and scarier than anything I had ever seen. I t was almost night again and there were lights on under the water glowing foamy otherworldly green.

We drove a few more miles and I must have dozed off again because I came awake with Matt's hand shaking me. I knuckled grit out of my eyes and stared at where he was pointing, which was just empty black desert. We came over a tiny crest in the road and then I had to blink and Haud and I were both hollering. What was ahead of us was Las Vegas at night and it came at us out of nowhere. Pale blackness, the faintest outline where the road met the sky, and then a carpet of impossibly brilliant jewel lights as far as I could see in either direction. It was like all the stars in the sky were scrunched together and then thrown on the desert floor, glittering marbles of light in swirls and patches and streams. The city threw a pink-orange bowl of light right back at the sky, the city said I have all your stars captured right here on the floor and I have the shine to prove it. Those stars living in the sky had gotten netted and dragged down to the desert to flower in the sand, and even in its hugeness the sky couldn't help feeling a little jealous of all that glory reflecting back at it. Not even a desert sky could absorb all the light that was Las Vegas, and we were going down into it.

Chapter 23

Cleaner, Brighter Whites

This is centrifugal force, Lore says. We are in the kitchen and she's holding a salad spinner. She turns the handle on top of a plastic barrel and a drum inside spins and then slows. As it spins, water flies from the lettuce and collects in drops to slide down the barrel. Centrifugal force is what makes the water come off the lettuce. This is different from gravity, which makes the water slide down the barrel. This is different from centripetal force as well.

The lettuce that I have just washed for supper is iceberg lettuce, pale green and ridged with thick white veins. We're making dinner. I took the lettuce from the drawer in the fridge that said Crisper. Another drawer said Meats and Cheeses and a small compartment with a hinged lid said Butter. This refrigerator can make ice cubes that come out of a spout when a lever is pressed. I hear the ice cubes dropping sometimes late at night when the house is quiet.

On the lettuce was a plastic net and I took this off and then carefully peeled the layers of leaves from the head and put them into a sink full of cold water. Lore said, Did you scrub the sink out first and I said yes but I hadn't, I didn't know we had to be THAT clean. I swished the leaves around and then Lore put them in the salad spinner. I washed tomatoes and cucumbers in the sink too and wondered did I have to change the water each time, and then decided no without asking Lore. Although she hums to herself while making dinner she can snap right away if you ask her a dumb question, her voice is dry and sharp and I get a cold feeling when she talks a certain way, like I'm naked and pinned to something and want to squirm.

The lettuce I cut into small pieces and put into a blue and white bowl that says Corningware pattern #710 on the bottom and which matches the other dishes in the cupboards. The tomatoes I cut into quarters and then eighths. I peel long strips of waxy skin from the cucumbers and then slice them into rounds, the knife going *thump* onto the cutting board. I first used to cut things by holding them in my hand and cutting against my thumb, but Lore said, Clane use the cutting board, I mean, really, I don't want you cutting yourself. I cut things this way without a board because that was how I did it when we lived in the field with Helene, I tried to explain. When we didn't have a kitchen. Well, you don't live in a field anymore, do you? Lore said. There's the cutting board, use it, and then clean it and put it away when you're finished. When the salad is done I put the bowl on the table in the dining room.

The kitchen gleams with white planes, the white counter tops, the refrigerator, the dishwasher, the stove with a convection oven. The no-wax linoleum floor that resists stains, scratches, scuffing, and fading. Fluorescent lights beam from the ceiling and light the underside of all the cupboards, which are also white and are filled with matching dishes and matching sets of pots and pans with no, I mean no, dried or burnt food clinging to the sides. The fridge has two compartments side by side, one is the freezer. The freezer is filled with rows of cans of apple and orange juice, bags of peas and carrots, and stacks of meat in styrofoam trays covered in plastic. There are pie crusts and cartons of cigarettes, Long 100s for Dean and Virginia Slims for Lore. Sometimes she smokes Benson & Hedges Ultra-Light 100s.

In this kitchen there's even a microwave, and Lore explained how it worked while Haud and I listened, fascinated. Waves of energy cross from one node to the other and they pass through the food sitting in between the two nodes. When the energy passes through the food it causes the molecules of the food to vibrate, and as the molecules vibrate they get hot from rubbing against each other. This is called friction. The faster a particle vibrates, the hotter it gets. This is why boiling water bubbles. And why ice cubes are solid.

Lore stands in front of the stove, a cigarette in one hand, her other hand resting on her hip. A strip of light from under the cupboard throws her face into sharp angles as she looks, frowning, into the oven. The oven has a light on inside and she is watching the dinner finish cooking, a pot roast bubbling inside of a Corningware pot with a clear lid. Lore is short and almost stout but not quite. She has blond hair cut short, and high hard cheekbones, and a nose hooked like an eagle's beak. She wears silk blouses open at the neck with scarves knotted there, and also around her neck are her glasses hanging on a gold chain. She wears them to see things up close and sometimes she looks at me over the rim of her glasses and this is her Oh really? look. She takes a drag off her cigarette and blows smoke upwards and turns around to the dining room and says, Dean, would you like wine?

Dean is reading the newspaper at the dinner table and he rattles it and says, That would be fine. Sometimes he has a martini and sometimes Lore has a gimlet. I know how to make martinis and gimlets for Dean and Lore. Dean is Lore's boyfriend, and he is a lawyer and Lore is a teacher. I ask Lore, Can I have a snack and Lore says, *May* I have a snack *please*, just take something from the crisper. I swear, you children act like you have been so deprived. I take a carrot and wander out of the kitchen and through the dining room and out of the sliding glass doors that go to the backyard.

In the backyard there is a fig tree and I look for figs while eating my carrot, chomping noisily now that I'm outside where Lore won't hear me. The figs are small and green and hard. Haud dared me to eat one but I didn't, I threw it at him, and it knocked over a vase on the patio table and I said, See what you made me do?

The fig tree has a broad green canopy of dense leaves and stands alone in the neatly mown yard. The grass is cut short, and beyond it is a cinderblock wall that encloses their property. Beyond the wall is an empty lot filled with the rubble of maybe a building that used to be there, clumps of mortar and cinderblocks in pieces and great big trenches. Haud and Matt ride dirt bikes over the humps and trenches sometimes, whooping and hollering. I can't see over the wall and don't feel like climbing over it, so I just lean against it, eating my carrot and listening to the sound of traffic going by far off in the evening air. The shape of the house behind me is neat and regular like all the houses in the neighborhood, no peeling paint or Indian-print curtains or swollen screen doors or broken cars in the driveway. The house is new and straight and the yard is always mowed and even the dog is neat, a Dalmatian named Lady, who doesn't have any personality that I know of and doesn't even shed. I throw my stub of carrot over the fence and turn back to the house, the lighted rectangles of the windows and sliding glass doors.

Haud is already at the table, swinging his legs and moving his fork around on his plate, playing invisible car and truck roadblock, No trucks passing, he says, stop or I'll shoot. That's no trespassing, I believe, Dean says from behind his paper. There are beads of moisture on Dean's wineglass and he folds up the paper and takes a drink. I slide into my place at the table and it's odd, very odd, to realize that this is my seat, where I'll always sit at this table, just like Dean has his and Lore has hers. Odd not in a bad way, but something I have to get used to. Like how the paper napkin, folded, with a knife and fork always goes on the left side of the plate, with the blade of the knife pointed toward the rim of the plate, and the spoon goes on the right, just under the different glasses for milk or water or wine or juice. You can't drink juice from a milk glass or water from a wineglass.

Lore is moving around in the kitchen and says, Clane would you please pour milk for yourself and Haud. Can I have juice instead? and she says, No, juice is for breakfast. I pour milk and Haud drinks some and Lore, placing the pot roast on the table, says, Haud wait for everyone to be seated. We are always doing little wrong things like this, drinking from the wrong glass or not setting the table right. Living with Lore means being corrected all of the time. On the other hand, there's all the food we want, all kinds, and there's TV. I've never had a TV before. I've never had any of this before. Glasses and plates and silverware that matches and a doorbell that rings and clean white wall-to-wall carpeting.

Dinner tonight is the salad I made with a dressing Lore made of oil and vinegar and oregano. There is the pot roast and potatoes and gravy and broccoli, all this food on my plate, I'm still surprised by it each time, I can have all of this and more too if I want it. A clean plate, and not a bowl I washed at the ditch. A plate that matches the other plates at the table, and salad bowls that match too. A fork and a spoon and a knife each time, not chopsticks. Pots on trivets and place mats at each place.

We hand Lore our plates and she dishes us slices of meat and mashed potatoes with a lake of gravy in the center. I help myself to broccoli and I can even put butter on it if I want to. I eat around the edges of the mashed potato mountain to keep the gravy lake from spilling. I put salt and pepper on everything and keep all the kinds of food separate on my plate. Haud pushes his fork through his potatoes, making roads and dams. Dean eats everything on his plate one kind at a time, first meat, then potatoes, then broccoli, then salad. Lore eats normal and snaps, fork raised halfway to her mouth, Good God Haud, must you play with your food? Eat it or wear it, Haud sings, slopping a fork of mashed potatoes onto his head, and I can't help it, I crack up at this, and we both lose our TV privileges for the night.

Chapter 24

Barbie's Dream House

I wake up because Haud is humming to himself. Across the room we share he is humped up under the covers on his bed, facing the wall, talking and humming. He says, This weekend only Youuu Ennn Elll Veee arena hosts young America's roughest toughest dirt bike championship ship ship ship. He has his hands cupped over his face and makes a rushing windy sound, wwrraaaaa and says, The crowd goes wild. Then he's quiet again and I know this means he's picking his nose and I also know he wipes the boogers in one place on the wall over his bed. He has a booger collection. Gold digger, I whisper loud, and he jerks guiltily. Lore's gonna kiiiiiill yoouuuu.

We share a room but we each have own our own beds, twin beds, with matching spreads. After our sleeping bags in the attic of Claude's, this is like Wow. I've never slept in a twin bed before. I've never slept in a room with matching twin beds. The curtains even match the bedspreads. Maybe they're not quite what I would have picked, they're a brown and blue and tan with baby blue flowers, but still, they're great. Each bed has a ruffled curtain around the bottom and this is called a dust ruffle. There are matching sheets and Lore shows me carefully how to make a bed correctly, the sheet with the pattern on the underside and the seam underneath so that when you fold the sheet down over the blanket you see the right side. I make the bed for hours. The pillowcases match.

In between our two beds we have a nightstand with a little drawer in it that holds a box of tissues and on top a little reading lamp for us to share. We have a whole closet to share, with mirrored doors and a big dresser with another mirror on top. There's a desk for studying. There's carpet on the floor and we have our own bathroom. This is the most amazing thing. The bathroom has a shower and a bathtub and matching towels in light blue. Bath towels AND hand towels. I wish there was someone I could tell this to, that we have our own bathroom. In my mind I can see the exclamation points that follow this sentence.

I lay in bed for a while thinking about not very much, watching the sunlight crawl up the wall, but then I remember it's Saturday and I'm up in a flash and digging for clothes. Cartoons, Haudie, I shout in a whisper, and he's scrambling for clothes too. We struggle silently into our clothes barely buttoning and zippering, barefoot, hair still clumped up from sleep, and we pad quickly into the kitchen for huge bowls of Apple Jacks. I had asked Lore would she buy Apple Jacks, and she did, after first reading the box. Can you believe that? She just went out and bought us Apple Jacks the very next time she went shopping, no lectures about sugar or imbalances in our system.

Haud switches on the little TV in the dining room, there's a bigger one in the living room but that's closer to Lore and Dean's room, and we drag our chairs up close to the screen and watch cartoons without moving or talking, our eyes never leaving the screen, not even to stretch or go to the bathroom. I even like the commercials. Barbie's Dream House, Slinky, Mongoose, Fashion Plates. There's Loony Tunes with Daffy Duck and Pepe Le Pew and Roadrunner and Wile E. Coyote and He-Man, Master of the Universe, and Superfriends, and George, George, George of the Jungle, watch out for that tree. Weak sunlight floats through the dining room curtains and moves silently across the floor, and the refrigerator makes ice cubes, and Lady walks carefully around the fig tree. M-I-C, see you real soon, K-E-Y, why, because we like you, M-O-U-S-E. Everything on TV shines.

Lore comes through the dining room on her way to the kitchen and we guiltily turn off the TV, knowing she'll say something if we keep it on. My body is stiff from sitting still so long and my eyes ache and Haud and I both stare blankly at the screen even though it's off. The silence of the house seems loud. Lore is making coffee for herself and Dean, smoking a cigarette in her robe. It's such a nice day, why don't you two go outside. The yard needs raking. And comb your hair, both of you.

Outside, the sky is a flat, far-off plane of not-quite-blue. It's not hot and not cold. I look for a rake in the garage and then begin to pile up leaves that have fallen on the lawn, first around the fig tree in the backyard. The backyard has the fig tree and a lawn of short stubby grass and a path of white gravel around the edges, where some uninterested-looking evergreen hedges grow. The cinderblock wall against the far end is another colorless kind of color that almost matches the sky. The house is long and low, with gray slate on the bottom half and gray siding on the top half.

From the front yard the house looks the same as it does in the back, and there's the same smooth flat lawn that is some shade of green that is not quite green and is springy like it's made of plastic, with one maple in the center. There's a garage for two cars, and more neat edges of white gravel planted with evergreens and cactus. The house is on a cul-de-sac, and the houses on each side look pretty much the same, different colors of slate or siding and different plants around the yard, but the same long low houses with slightly overhanging eaves and aluminum window frames and wide low steps. No trees along the street, but clumps of cactus and grasses as tall as trees, and box hedges. The street is wide and smooth and sleek, no bumps or potholes or patches or cracks or tree roots. Each house number is painted neatly on the sidewalk in front. No sounds come from any houses, but far down the street a door opens and closes, a car leaves quietly, a sprinkler starts on someone's lawn. I don't know if there are any kids on this street, I haven't seen any, but we haven't been here that long yet.

Lady comes politely around the house and wags her tail a little, looking at me with a question in her eyes. Haud comes flying around the house from the other side yelling, Nana nana

nana nana Bat-maaaan, nobody knows who you are, and flings himself into the pile of leaves I just raked. That's Spiderman, stupid, I say. We rake up the pile again and put the leaves in bags and then in the trash can where Lore told us to. The sky is all surface and this is how you rake leaves, I'm thinking, the only detail in my mind. Then we go in the house for breakfast.

Pancakes and bacon and orange juice and milk. Eat a balanced breakfast with orange juice from Florida every day. Lore says, Go put your jacket away, Clane, it doesn't belong on the back of your chair, I mean, really. This is the dining room, not your bedroom. The dining room drapes are open now and sunlight, the same pale color as the orange juice, slants across the table, a glare bouncing off the dishes and glassware. Maybe it's the glare in my eyes after too much TV or maybe it's that I ate six pieces of bacon and four pancakes drenched in syrup, but I feel sick and I groan, I'm stuffed. Don't say stuffed, Clane, that's vulgar. Say I'm finished may I be excused please. If she thinks that's vulgar, what would she think about Helene saying shitpissfuck or I don't give a flying fuck. Please clear the table if you're finished, Clane. Dean rattles his paper and Lore pours more coffee and gets papers out to grade and I carry dishes from the table to the sink. I scrape them into the disposal and rinse them and put them in the dishwasher and turn the dishwasher on. Dean and Lore are rich, I think, to have two TVs and a dishwasher and a washer and dryer and two cars. The dishwasher hums and I'm glad I know how to do these things now, use the garbage disposal, turn on the dishwasher. Raking leaves, making my bed, setting the table, these things mean I have a normal life now. I don't change clothes inside my sleeping bag to stay warm or grind rice flour sitting on a rock in a field or swish gravel in the dishes to clean them. I wipe down the counters for Lore and she says, Thank you, Clane, that will be all.

I'm standing in front of the sink, wiping my hands on my pants, with Lore looking at me critically, and I'm thinking, Uh-oh, here it comes, don't use your pants to dry your hands, use a dishtowel, but she turns her head to the side, her hands on her hips, and says, How many pairs of pants do you have, Clane, maybe three? I shrug. I have these, which are my corduroys, and my overalls, and still the green bell bottoms that I have to wear a long shirt over to cover the hole in the butt. Let's go to your room, she says, and I follow, reluctantly, because I don't know if I'm in trouble or what for yet. I pull open the drawer of the dresser with my clothes, embarrassed because they're not folded, but she doesn't seem to notice, ruffling through my holey shirts and mismatched socks. The small piles look sad in the bottom of the almost empty drawer. Hmm, let's get you some new clothes, Lore says. you're going to need them for your new school. Huge exclamation marks fill my head. I've got school supplies for you but you need new clothes. She says this matter-of-fact like it's no big deal but inside me is a glowing spreading warmth. I don't know if this means she likes me, that she's going to buy me clothes, and that's why I'm glad, or if I'm glad to just be getting new clothes, but either way I'm glad.

Lore gets her purse and cigarettes, which she keeps in a little snap purse thingy, and her sunglasses. Haud and I race for the car, he gets shotgun. Lore drives carefully, hunched up close to the steering wheel, both hands on it, signaling at every turn even if there's no one behind her, stopping at every stop sign. I wedge myself between the two front seats to watch where we're going, excited, but Lore says, For God's sake Clane sit where you're supposed to, and I sit back, abashed, now looking out of the passenger seat window. We don't sing in the car with Lore. We're going to Mervyn's. I've never been to Mervyn's though I saw one once in Santa Rosa, a big cement box surrounded by miles of parking lots. I can go to Mervyn's now, I think, because I'm riding in a car. If I was with Helene, first of all we'd never go to Mervyn's except maybe to steal. If we did we'd walk, and there's something funny about walking, and barefoot too, across a long parking lot. I'd feel like a bug about to be squashed. A hippie bug. If I was with Claude we'd be in his truck and then I'd feel like a hippie redneck. But in Lore's new-looking station wagon and all of us in shoes and Lore even in heels and with her hair done we can go to Mervyn's. I'm going to get clothes that are really new.

Mervyn's is huge, just like Kmart, miles of aisles, brightly lit, refrigerated, with soft music playing over the loudspeakers. Really g-a-y music, Beatles songs On violins without the words. Haud and I bounce down the aisles, skipping and slapping our shoes on the linoleum floor. We pass cages of huge beach balls and pool toys. No, Lore says firmly, her mouth pressed tight. We pass bicycles and Big Wheels and roller skates. No, Lore says more sharply. We're looking for clothes, c-l-o-t-h-e-s, she spells grimly. She steers me to the Girls section and says, Pick out what you think you'll need. Please be sensible. She marches Haud to the Boys section, hand firmly clamped on his shoulder.

I shuffle though racks of blouses, sweaters, dresses. I peel layers of turtlenecks apart and run my hands over rows of skirts and then sundresses and then long dresses. Circular racks of jeans and corduroys and shorts. My heart is thumping in my chest and I almost can't breathe. I'm dizzy and confused, overwhelmed by the variety of colors and shapes and sizes. Am I XS, S, M, L, or XL? Size 8, or 10, or 12 or 12 XS or 12M? Each kind of clothes has a different kind of size. Skirts are just letters but pants are number and letters. Lore comes back and I haven't picked anything out and she's exasperated. I pick some things, fast, not looking too carefully at what they are. A pink skirt, pink socks, green blouse, yellow shirt. It's like I'm seeing through a tunnel. Everything is too bright, colors wash and blur around me, I get lost in the aisles, clothes slip off the racks and they fall out of my arms and I trip over the hangers. I make a pile of clothes in a basket that Lore brings me and we look for Haud.

We pass fuzzy sweaters and ski jackets and plaids and Accessories and flowers and solids and prints and Matching Separates and Career Wear. Stripes and polka dots and shirts that say Hang in There Baby and Keep On Truckin' and Smile and Pobody's Nerfect. Down the aisles other families are doing the same thing, arguing, pulling clothes off racks, sitting down in the aisles to try on shoes or socks. I want one that says Star Trek, I want the one that says Trekkie, I want the blue one, you got the red one. Moms are chasing little kids and dragging them out, howling, from under racks. Girls are holding blouses up to their chests, How about yellow, isn't this cuuuute? We find Haud wandering through Ladies Intimates with a bra on his head, dragging a Spiderman sweatshirt by the hood, butting through racks of clothes, knocking over boxes of shoes.

While Lore furiously whispers to Haud, I'm back in the Juniors section watching two girls try shorts on under their skirts. They have baskets full of filmy, delicate clothes and when they see me looking at them they turn to each other and whisper and then turn away. They're both tall and blond with long hair held up by ponytail holders with fuzzy balls on them. They're wearing pretty, stripey dresses and have dangly earrings and bracelets. They're chattering and arguing and gurgling *coo cooo whooo oooo* sounds. I wanted this one when I saw Misty has one too and now we can match. One holds up a blouse with butterflies on it, and the other one goes, Awwww that's so suuuper. I look down at myself in my holey pants and I've forgotten to put my shoes back on and my zipper is down, and who knows maybe I have huge bugs crawling all over me or leaking sores or something. My face is all hot. The clothes in Juniors are all too big for me but now I'm lost. I hate everything I picked. This isn't fair, I'm thinking. The first time I ever get to pick new clothes, not from the free box, anything I want, but I can't pick because my mind is blank, just blank, gone. I can feel Lore waiting for me, impatiently wanting a cigarette, so I don't take the time to try anything on. She asks are your sure you have the right sizes and I just nod dumbly, my eyes darting helplessly around the kaleidoscope.

At the checkout line I hand her my choices. Skirts and pants and blouses and socks and a jacket and a turtleneck. She adds tennies she picked up and sandals. She has a pile for Haud, Garanimals and Toughskins and tennies and socks and sweatshirts. Haud comes clomping toward us in huge snakeskin cowboy boots, and Lore puffs out a huge sigh and rolls her eyes to the ceiling. I'm silent in the car on the way home. My mind is tumbling with different clothes just like a washer and dryer. I see a part of this for an instant and a part of that for an instant and then another part goes by and another and then a falling blur and then another.

Chapter 25

Oil of Olay

There are all these things I have to learn about what is a normal life. The next one is about Cleanliness.

Haud and I come in for dinner and right away we get a Look. Lore has so many Looks I'm learning to identify them. There is the Oh, Reeeeally, as in, are you sure you're going to build a tree house in the fig tree? There is the Oh REALLY, as in, Claude never made you brush your teeth, but you'll brush them every day when you're in this house. There is the one like, Egad, look at the dirt under your fingernails, and the What Did I Do to Deserve This? During dinner we get the Oh Please with the cocked head. Go wash your hands before dinner, how many times have I had to tell you that?

We had been in the yard trying to get Lady to understand the idea that a ball was for chasing if you were a dog. Lady was a dog that was puzzled by this. She was a nice dog but as far as dog personalities that's all she was. We showed her the ball, a tennis ball, and she looked at it and her tail moved a little and she tilted her ears up. A minute went by and her tail moved again, hesitantly. Go get it Lady, I said, and threw the ball. Lady yawned and sat down. Rub it around her mouth, Haud said helpfully. We gotta show her how. I held her between my legs and pried her

mouth open and Haud tried to stuff the ball between her teeth.
Lady sneezed and with a look that I swear was apologetic she
went to lie down in the sun by the door, but Haud tackled her and
rolled around on the grass with her while she scrambled madly to
get out from under him.

So we were full of dog hairs and leaves and grass when we
went in to dinner and that's when we got the Oh Please. Go wash
up. We shoved each other down the hall and shoved getting in the
door and shoved at the bathroom sink. Fucker, Haud said.
Shitface, I said. Quietly. Lore doesn't like swearing.

At the table, Lore is setting wineglasses down in front of
her place and Dean's and milk glasses in front of me and Haud.
Dean takes his face out of the paper and folds it neatly and puts it
on the sideboard behind him and then unfolds his napkin and
beams in the general direction of the fried chicken Lore is passing
around. I look at my chicken, not sure if I'm supposed to eat it
with a knife and fork, thinking that seems silly, but not wanting to
do it wrong and have Lore get all hyper. She says, almost kindly
and with a humor I'm beginning to understand is dry, Among
polite company it's perfectly acceptable to eat fried chicken with
one's hands, Clane. Haud is already gobbling at his and says, In
medieval times nobody had silverware and they ate everything
with their hands and threw things. Let's not go that far, shall we?
Lore says around her drumstick. I pick up my piece and very
delicately take bites and think I'm doing pretty good. Lore's gaze
can be like barbed wire sometimes. I try to slip beneath the wire

of that gaze without getting snagged on it. I brush a lock of hair out of my eyes and Lore says, For god's sake Clane wipe your hands first, and very quickly without thinking I wipe my hands on my pants and Lore winces and rolls her eyes up to the ceiling in a double whammy of Egad and What Did I Do to Deserve This.

I swear, sometimes I think your mother and father raised you both as wolves, Lore continues, but just conversationally as she keeps eating. I visited your mother and father just after you were born, Clane, you know. Lore puts salad into a bowl for herself and passes the salad bowl to Haud. The three of you were living in a storefront in San Francisco in absolute squalor. It was appalling, and she says it like appaaaalling. You were crawling around on the floor without diapers and eating things off the floor. She says it like eeeaating. Lore carefully peppers her salad and takes a bite. My fork is stopped in midair, I'm just listening, not eating, interested. I don't have any baby pictures of myself and I've never heard Claude or Helene say anything about when I was a baby. Lore says, I said to Helene, you might clean the floor once in a while, you know, and Helene just shrugged in that offhand way of hers and said, Why bother, it'll just get dirty again. My God, Lore said. Your mother thought it was simply too bourgeois to clean. She wanted to live naturally, you see. Lore laughs to the ceiling again. But even animals clean themselves, she went on. There are schools of fish that follow whales, and do you know why? Because they feed off the barnacles that grow on whales. Small fish clean these whales. Cleanliness and order are built into nature.

When we're all done eating and we've asked to be excused Lore asks us to clear the table and scrape the dirty dishes in the garbage disposal and load the dishwasher and wipe the counters. Haud pours gobs of Comet on the counters and swipes it around in piles while I hiss at him and kick him in the shins. Don't, Lore's gonna get mad again. Lore comes into the kitchen and with one hand holding a cigarette aloft and with the other hand cupping her elbow she looks critically at us, a little like the way she did when she asked us about clothes. Just out of curiosity, she says, Do you even own a toothbrush? I nod, slowly, still absently wiping extra Comet off the counter and trying to kick a small pile of it that's on the floor under the counter where she won't see it. Carol and Larry bought us toothbrushes, I say. How often do you brush your teeth? Reluctantly I shrug, and say, like it's a question, Twice a day? And how often do you bathe? Lore asks, dragging fiercely on her Virginia Slim. I shrug again, now lost. What's the right thing to say? I haven't really bathed since we got here, maybe splashed around in the tub once or twice because I was so impressed with the washcloths matching the towels. Do you mean to tell me, and she drags again and blows a plume of smoke, do you mean to tell me that no one has bothered to inform you that people generally bathe twice a week on a regular basis? She says bathe like baaaaathe and her voice is rising into an Egad. I shake my head, my toe moving in the patch of Comet. Well, this is something you must do. You and Haud need to bathe a minimum of twice a week, WITH soap, WITH shampoo. I don't care if you use the tub or the shower but I want you to clean yourselves regularly, and to be in the habit of this before school starts. She says absently to the ceiling, My GOD I hope you don't have lice. I don't, I say quickly, anxious to watch TV. Tomorrow I'll take you two for haircuts, she says.

She takes us to the beauty parlor where she has her hair done. It's close to the house in a mall of slightly mean-looking small low buildings that look like they're trying to hide from the Nevada sun. A lot of the buildings in Las Vegas look like this, the smaller ones, not the bigger ones. Low to the ground, painted mostly gray or white or tan, on bumpy asphalt lots. Buildings that look like afterthoughts, built only for function, with tired shrubs in small patches of gravel.

The beauty shop has rows of pink sinks and reclining vinyl swivel chairs that raise and lower. There's a wall of mirrors marbled in gold streaks and a lot of ladies in pink smocks sitting under huge hair driers, smoking and reading magazines. When we walk in Lore says, Hello Norine, these are my grandchildren. Please give them each a trim and I'll have my usual treatment. Lore digs a cigarette from her purse while settling into a chair as a smock is draped around her. A woman with tired eyes and frosted hair guides Haud into a chair and pins a towel around his neck and snaps a smock over him. In the mirrors he looks like a little ratty dog wearing a pink tent. He scowls and kicks at the chair and bounces in his seat while the woman struggles to comb the knots out of his long hair, jerking at the ends while he grumps, Ow ow ow. When she finishes he looks even funnier, with his hair hanging flat but ragged like a mop. She bends his head backward over a little sink and tests the warmth of the water against her wrist and then shampoos him vigorously and dries his hair a little with a towel. By now I am howling with silent laughter because when Norine takes his head out from under the towel he looks just like a mad wet cat. *Snick, snick, snick,* hunks of hair fall all over his lap and onto the floor, and then she blows his hair dry and combs it again and he looks at himself in the mirror, all sleek and shining, his hair still a little long, touching his collar and with bangs. You look like Prince Valiant, I say.

I sit still while Norine wraps me. Her fingers feel cool and efficient on my neck. She combs my hair out, and hanging down across my chest it looks longer than I thought it was. She turns me to face myself in the mirror and runs her fingers through my hair and says, We'll just take these dry ends off. I look at myself in the mirror, eyes too big in my small dark face, mouth and nose too big, not a dainty little mouth and a pointy little nose or blue eyes, no winning smile, my face creased by a frown at how dark and ugly I am, a gypsy face.

I've never gotten my hair cut at a beauty parlor and I sit very still and if I didn't have to look at my face I would like this. Norine's fingers massage my scalp pleasantly and I think of Debbie washing my hair over the sink in Ojo Sarco and I realize again how no woman ever touches me, no soft warm mothery sistery hands are ever on me. Lore doesn't hug and I wouldn't want her to, anyway. Just this tired lady in a beauty shop. Her hips brush my arms where they rest on the chair. Do I move them from beneath her or stay still? I wonder. I stay still and her hips are soft and solid and comforting. *Snick snick* and there's piles of my hair on the floor. When she's done I look the same only neater and cleaner, and I'm filled with deep disappointment. I thought a haircut would change me.

At home I go to the mirror in the bathroom again and again all day to see if I look any different. In our bedroom I lay out all my new clothes and then I fold them carefully and place them neatly in my drawers. I have new clothes and a new haircut and a clean bathroom anytime I want to use it and a chest of drawers and a closet to put my clothes in and a washer and dryer and an iron and an ironing board too. I feel like I have to take advantage of all this.

When no one is around I carefully explore the bathroom. In the cabinet over the sinks there are vials and bottles and jars and tubes and I look into each one, skin lotion that smells like almonds and calamine lotion and Vaseline and toothpaste. Under the sink there are more bottle and jars, old stuff of Lore's that's half used up. Cloudy bottles of nail polish and nail-polish remover, dried-up face lotion and eye cream, Oil of Olay caked thickly on the bottom of a blue plastic container, a layer on the lid dried and cracking. Pepto-Bismol and cough syrup, both of which

I taste cautiously. I open up and look at and smell everything, sitting crosslegged on the bathroom rug. A tub of bath powder that smells like dusty flowers, Doan's Foot Rub, cakes of Ivory Soap 99.9% Pure. Shampoos and conditioners, some matching, mostly used up. I put fresh cakes of soap in the tub and shower and by the sink, and all the bottles of shampoo and conditioner on the rim of the tub. I shake a whole bag of old makeup out onto the rug and carefully pore over and smell and test all of it, face powder and foundation and eyeliner, mascara that I get into my eyes, lipstick that I get on my teeth, blush and eye shadow. I paint my toenails and get polish on everything. I soak cotton ball after cotton ball in the remover and scrub it all off, a little old lady color of pinkish tan.

Now I shower every single night using whole palmfuls of shampoo and conditioner. I blow my hair dry, and half the day I run into the bathroom to spray it with Aqua Net and flip it around. I try side parts and middle parts. I bend over and fluff it out and flip it back and spray it more, until it's first big and fluffy and then clumps into huge thick crusty hunks. It looks beyond ridiculous and I shower again and wash it out and I look at myself in the shower, water beading up and running down my flat chest. I have two black hairs over my veejay now and two hard bumps on my chest like a mosquito bite gets when you scratch it too much. I pat face powder all over my cheeks and put concealer under my eyes and then wash it off quick when I hear Lore padding down the hall to call dinner time. I try on different outfits with different socks to match my skirts and different shirts to match my pants, and I iron rigid creases into everything. I fold and refold my clothes and arrange and rearrange them in the drawers and run into the closet to look at my clothes all day.

School is going to start on Monday. We got a thing in the mail that has a map of my new school and the room numbers I have to go to at different times of day and a map of the bus route. I will be going to North Las Vegas Junior High in the fifth grade.

Chapter 26
Kimberly Jennifer Anne

On the night before the first day of school Lore shows me
how to set the alarm clock and we set it for seven a.m. I'm up in a
flash almost before it goes off. I basically didn't sleep all night. I
carefully put on the clothes I ironed the night before, a pink and
maroon skirt, pink socks, sandals. I brush my hair again and
again. Haud is up too and we gobble cereal while watching
cartoons. Lore is grumbling around the kitchen in a robe and she
gives us lunch money and watches while we zip it into the back
pockets of our new backpacks. Mine also holds my new school
supplies, a notebook and a spiral binder and a zippered pouch of
pencils and erasers and a ruler and scissors. So much new stuff,
light bouncing of the red plastic of my binder, a crisp manila
folder, even a new comb so my hair won't be messy before class.

All the way to the bus stop I worry. What if I'm late?
What if there was a time change and I forgot about it? What if
the bus route is wrong? What if I'm on the wrong corner? When
the bus comes my chest is tight with anxiousness. The bus squeaks
to a halt in front of me and I climb in nervously and scan the
length of the bus for an empty seat, scared to sit next to someone
I don't know. I slide into a seat near the window and watch as we
move off.

The bus is almost empty but it fills up quickly when we stop at other places. Three girls flounce on, giggling, and two of the girls slide into the seat ahead of me and the third stops at my seat and looks at me and kind of wrinkles her nose but slides in next to me and then plumps her backpack down to make a barrier between us. She leans over the seat and whispers excitedly to the girls in front of us and they all ignore me completely while I look out the window some more.

The bus bumps over some railroad tracks and leaves the part of the city that's all houses, and the road stretches out into empty lots and barren patches and small ugly stores and malls. At another bump the girls all look at me and their faces seem too close to mine, everything bright with nervousness and morning sun. The girl next to me pulls out a little purse with a matching brush and flips her hair over to comb it and shakes her hair down into a perfect flip style. Then a matching compact and lip gloss, she puts it on expertly while the bus is moving and I stare at her in awe. All the girls are talking excitedly until they notice me looking and one looks at me like, WHAT do you want? I look hurriedly out the window again. Watermelon is the best Lip Smackers flavor, they are saying, But for gloss I like strawberry Bonne Bell best. Not grape, grape is gross. Jennifer, let me use your comb, okay? one girl is saying, and Kimberly, do you think my highlights are showing up? another is saying, and Stop spazzing. I can't get my eyeliner on straight, another is saying. One of the girls looks back at me and says, What's your name?

Clane, I say, the syllable coming out like a blunt single clump, not lilty like Kimberly or elegant like Jennifer or simple like Anne. At my name all three stop what they're doing and look at me and ask, Where did you get a name like THAT? I start to explain about Claude—Clod like a clod of dirt? one asks in shocked disbelief —and Helene but the bus rolls into the parking lot and everyone is scrambling out and no one waits for me to finish.

I cross the long parking lot lined with buses idling white smoke, spilling kids out onto the pavement. Everyone is yelling and calling to each other. I stumble over a curb and bang into a boy and lose my balance and clutch for a minute at his sleeve and he shrugs me off impatiently and says, What's that gunk all over your face? With my heart thudding I push through the front doors and go into the girls' bathroom and look in the mirror. My hair is a flat hank of fur crusted with hairspray and the powder I put on my face is smeared unevenly across my cheeks and the brown eye shadow I used looks like patches of dirt. I scrub my face desperately with a wet paper towel, shoved out of the way by a gaggle of girls screeching and calling and adjusting their clothes and swinging their purses and slamming the stall doors. You're such a dog, I say to myself in the mirror when everyone's gone, and I'm late for my first class. You're such a dog.

Chapter 27

Tangent Radius Arc

School. I stand on the edge of the playground at recess, a vast plain of concrete with tetherballs slapping in the distance. The wind whips whorls of grit from a vacant lot through a chain link fence that surrounds the school complex. The empty desert beyond is all blank space except for low dunes and weeds. I hook my fingers into the chain and lean into the wind, watching the tumbleweeds shiver and move and gather in low spots and along the fence. I watch other kids running, their indistinct shouts floating on the air. At the very edge of the playground the buildings of the school stretch out low on the ground beneath the aluminum sky. The buildings are just a dark smudge from where I am and I can barely hear the bell ring after recess that means break is over. I start back across the mile of weedy cracked concrete, five minutes to be back in class.

My pack slaps against me as I half-run half-trot to class. I keep my backpack on all of the time because even though we have lockers to store our stuff I can almost never get the combination to work and after being late a few times and not knowing who to ask to fix it, I gave up. The binder has stuff in it now, the folders have papers in them, but the zippered plastic pouch I never use, or any of the stuff in it.

I trudge across the last few feet of the lot and scoot across the passageway leading to the gym, which is a shortcut to math. A huge banner stretches across the gym, saying, Fall is here, welcome back to school, with pictures of falling leaves and footballs and stacks of books. It's supposed to mean now it's time for sweaters and football games and school again, this is what fall means. I'm not sure if I knew that before. Fall is back-to-school time. Get your fuzzy sweater out.

The weather doesn't feel like fall, though, and there aren't any football games that I know of. It's hot and dry every day and a wind worries around the corners of the prefabs and goes whipping through the halls if the door is open too long. The sky is the color of metal and the leaves on the trees haven't changed or dropped. The gymnasium is the biggest school building I've ever seen. At registration on the first day of school I stood in a line with about a million other kids, and still the gym seemed too big even for all of us. I had to wait in one line to sign a list that had my name and age and address, and then another line to find out my homeroom and schedule. I didn't know a single person in the whole building or a single thing of what was happening and had to just wait and worry and maybe think of asking some other kid for help but not actually do it. Is this the right line for new students? Is this the right line for A through H? What line is for fifth graders? which line is for sixth graders? Am I in fifth or sixth grade? I forget. What line is for A lunch and which is for B lunch? Because so many kids go here they have to have lunch at different times. That was the first day, and nothing about it was even a little bit okay.

Through the gym, which is empty right now and take a right across the breezeway and turn left at the second bungalow and go father down the row to B-12. This is my English class. There are streams of kids all around me moving in all directions, flashes of color from jackets and shirts and sweaters, sneakers and loafers and sandals slapping the pavement. The purple sweatshirt with the hood is Danny,the cutest boy at school, and the yellow wind breaker is Dana, but I don't say hi to either one of them. Not to Danny because I saw him kissing a girl and they both had their mouths open and their eyes closed. Not to Dana because she was in a line behind me at the snack bar and after I bought a pickle and took a bite out of it she said how I eat my pickles is gross. It's not gross, I said. I eat the crunchy outside part but I don't like the mushy inner part where all the seeds are.

Luckily I don't have Dana in this English class. I have her in a Social Studies class. I met her when we were supposed to get to know the person to our left. I said hi and she said hi and she said, Where are you from? I didn't know whether to say California or New Mexico so I said, I live with my grandmother and her boyfriend. Dana said, You mean they're not married? and I was stuck again. Dana asked where was my mom and dad, and I made something up quick. Dana is from Wisconsin. Her dad is a mining engineer and her mom is an accountant.

I pull open the door to the classroom, which is metal and heavy and closes with a very definite clunk. In this class we have assigned seats, which in a way is good since I don't have to worry about where to sit. I just go to my desk, which is part of a very straight row of desks in a very straight classroom. Mrs. Tedesco likes it that way and straightens the desks I think every day. I slide into my seat and shrug off my jacket and pull out my textbook and my binder and arrange them carefully with a new pencil. I can't use a pen yet because my penmanship is awful. I never knew you're supposed to write in cursive. I can't do cursive. But I have read most of the way through my textbook already and don't even have to pay attention in class. In fact I do much better if I don't pay attention. I found this out right away. This belongs in my long list of things I've found out about straight schools that make them way different from hippie schools.

What we were supposed to have read this week for homework was "The Red Pony" by John Steinbeck which I read a long time ago. I also read his book called *Cannery Row* and *Tortilla Flats* and *Of Mice and Men*, all of which Lore has in her big bookcase in the living room.

Let's open our textbooks to page eighty-three, Mrs. Tedesco is saying. She has wiry curly gray hair and looks like a dyke. That's a new word I learned at school. Mrs. Tedesco walks around the room with something between a strut and a waddle.

People, raise your hands, she's saying. What was the meaning of this story by Steinbeck? No one raises their hand.

Behind me two boys are kicking each other under their desks and beside me three girls are trading notes and another girl is brushing her hair in quick furtive strokes, holding the brush in her lap so Mrs. Tedesco doesn't see it. She turns now and surveys the class from the front of the room. I have my hand up but she doesn't call on me. She never calls on me because I always have my hand up and I always know the answers in this class. I always raise my hand even though she won't call on me because I feel sorry for her that no one pays any attention to her. As she turns away the girl with the hairbrush gives the curls along her head a quick flip. They stand out from her face like wings and the next time Mrs. Tedesco is looking away the girl takes a tiny hairspray out of her purse and sprays the wings and fluffs them gently.

"The Red Pony" was a good story but it isn't taking up enough room in my head so I'm thinking about other things while the teacher talks. "The Red Pony" is about a boy who must come to terms with the loss of a thing he loves, the teacher is saying. This is called a coming-of-age story, as the protagonist goes from being a boy to becoming a man. Mrs. Tedesco says this and I am half listening to her but half thinking about something else, starvation, desperation, and confused and angry Japanese peasants who are thin and ragged, from a movie I once saw with Helene. I'm thinking about the desperate anguish of a town of peasants who will starve if bandits raid their rice crop again. A group of samurai men save the town, and one of the men chases a young boy down a hill only to find that the boy is actually a girl.

Her father cut her hair off so she'd be mistaken for a boy and not be raped by the bandits or the samurai. The girl falls in love with the samurai who uncovers her secret.

I am thinking about this while I watch the girl finish patting her hair. Mrs. Tedesco is saying, What we learn from this story is the fact of our own mortality. We realize that each of us will face loss and that the ultimate loss is death. I look at my fingernails, which I wish would grow out but they always grow out sideways instead of long. Mortality doesn't mean a thing to me, and what I call loss is a big shapeless thing not connected to the loss of any one thing except maybe my sister. Loss is the line of poplar trees along the road around the trailer park with the sun slanting through them, loss is the sound crickets make at dusk. Mrs. Tedesco says, Take out a sheet of paper and write your name and the date in the upper right hand corner.

Math class is next and is in one of the little trailer rooms, the bungalows, the prefabs, temporary classrooms except that they look like they've been temporary for the last twenty years. In math class we can sit where we want and this is just one of many problems connected to math class. Do I sit next to the boy with the short black hair because he let me borrow an eraser and take the risk of him thinking I'm following him, which I'm not? It's more like I'm escaping from everyone else than following him. Do I sit next to the really fat girl because no one else will, but is that too much loser per square inch, her and me? If I sit too far from the blackboard I can't see the problems, but if I sit too close I have to smell the teacher. Mr. Shank chain-smokes and the smell of him is like a dense, rank, moist cloud. I'll just sit in the middle of the room, where not many people like to sit because the teacher can see them all from his desk and they can't goof off as much.

For math class I need my textbook and my workbook and my binder, and here's another problem, because I can't balance them all on my desk. I have to have all three because one has the problems and another has how the problems are done and the third has to show all my work. The panicky feeling is starting to set in already. I'm never prepared for math because the truth is I don't know math, hardly any of it beyond addition and subtraction and some multiplication but not even long division and really really not the geometry and pre-algebra we're supposed to be learning in this class.

Lore looked at a test I brought home that I failed and she was livid. For the life of me I do not understand how you could have failed to learn your multiplication tables, Clane. But I never did any math in free school, I whined. Well, you're going to learn some math now, she said grimly. No TV, no playing outside, no games, no music until you memorize your multiplication tables all the way up to nine times nine. For a week I used the flash cards she gave me and when she quizzed me I only passed because at the dining room table where we went over them there was enough light shining through the cards for me to see the answers on the back.

What we're supposed to know now, arc and tangent and radius and diameter and angles and pi and solving for x is a language I don't understand at all. Math is its own language and it's one I don't speak. Mr. Shank's voice comes from way off as he stands at the board going over stuff. My vision narrows into a pinpoint as I try not to cry and then not to slam my book shut and scream that I don't understand. I did that once and the whole class stopped dead still and looked at me. What! I yelled at the whole class. No wonder no one talks to me. Papers and books in front of me go blurry with tears and my eyes ache from not letting the tears spill over. I have to take some deep breaths. After looking at the problems looking back at me for some nameless amount of time I just start drawing doodles on my notebook and my frustration eases itself into a dreaming kind of boredom.

Chapter 28

Friday, October 6, is Cheeseburgers, Tater Tots, and Carrot Salad

Cinnamon toast you eat by taking bites all around the outside edge of the toast. You have to save the best part, the soggy buttery part in the middle, for last. The less-tasty crispy outer part of cinnamon toast is what keeps it toast instead of just a handful of sog.

You make cinnamon toast by first spreading two slices of bread with plenty of butter, or three pieces if Lore's not home to remind you not to spoil your appetite for dinner. White bread is better for this because it soaks up the butter more and is the right combination of chewy and soft, but then the butter has to be room temperature or you tear holes in the bread. Then pour on sugar, being careful not to get it on the floor. White pours better but brown tastes better. Then sprinkle on cinnamon and put the slices in the toaster oven. Put the toaster oven on Broil and not on Toast because it makes better toast if the underside isn't toasted. Watch the toast while you're waiting, because if you don't watch it and instead go back to the TV you'll forget and the sugar burns easy. It doesn't take that long, but when you're really hungry for cinnamon toast it takes way too long. Watch with your arms crossed on the counter and your chin on your arms. When you can't stand it anymore hop up and down and sing, Toast toast toast toast toast toast toast toast to the tune of *Wheel of Fortune*.

Cheese toasties you make not with toast but with crackers. Start by putting a grid of crackers down on the counter, square ones like Wheat Thins. Cut tiny pieces of cheese, one for each cracker, and cut the cheese (get it, cut the cheese?) against the ball of your thumb because it takes too long to get out the cutting board and besides your crackers are all over the counter and there's no room for the cutting board, which would just be another thing to wash anyway. Add little pieces of onion to each cracker, but for this you really do need the cutting board or your hands will smell like onion all day. So use garlic salt instead. Also put a drop of Tabasco on each cracker. Carefully carry each cracker to the microwave. Watch the microwave the same way you watch the toaster but be careful of the waves. Haud says, They can come out and cook your brain.

Toaster-oven pizza you make by splitting an English muffin and spreading tomato sauce on each half and then you add cheese and then into the toaster oven. You can leave it in there longer than cinnamon toast, long enough to go outside and toss a ball for Lady even though she won't catch it, or long enough to go back to the *Brady Bunch* for a minute, but not long enough for the next commercial or you'll burn it. I've burned a lot of toaster-oven pizza this way.

With toaster-oven pizza the middle is sometimes mushy from the sauce, and the way to avoid this is to toast the muffin first, then add the sauce and cheese, and then toast it again. If it gets too toasted you'll burn the roof of your mouth eating it. The first time I ever made toaster-oven pizza I had to stop and think. Cheese first or sauce first? When I added other stuff, salami, I had to think again. Sauce and then cheese and then stuff? or sauce and then stuff and then cheese?

Lore gives us fifty cents every day for school lunch, but sometimes I make my own lunch and then save the lunch money for other things, like pickles at the snack bar. Snack bar pickles you eat by first double-wrapping the pickle in a napkin, leaving the top part open. Then you take small careful bites from the top and then the outside of the pickle, the crispy part, avoiding the slick slippery pickle guts, which you throw out or put down the back of Haud's collar or try to get Lady to eat. Do the same thing with raw carrots—eat the outside edge and leave the core, just to see if you can. How to eat tomatoes is whole, like apples, but with salt. The salt won't stick on the tomato before the first bite, so lick it first, then salt it, then salt each bite. How to eat cucumbers is with the bottle of vinegar in your other hand. Take a bite of cucumber and then a swig of vinegar. Don't let anyone catch you drinking vinegar from the bottle. How to eat grapes is either carefully peel them with your fingernails, and then gross out on how slick they are, like eyeballs, or put them in your nose and then shoot them out when you pretend to sneeze. How to eat grapefruit is first cut it in half, then cut around the inside to loosen the fruit from the rind, then sprinkle it with sugar, and then use a special spoon that has ridged edges to cut out each section of fruit. I didn't even know there was such a thing as grapefruit spoons. I didn't know about egg cups, either, or steak tartare or McDonald's cherry pies or how waffles are really good with bacon on them. All of this we've learned being here at Lore's. We were like little animals before. Lore says we're still like little animals.

When we first got here we went through the fridge and ate everything. We ate the olives with pimientos stuffed in them for Dean's martinis, and the Maraschino cherries for Lore's Manhattans, and the capers and the pickled onions and the bread-and-butter pickles. We ate a whole Boston cream pie from the freezer and slice after slice of American cheese. Lore was flabbergasted. She said that. She said, My god I'm flabbergasted. You children are like little animals. Anything that didn't need to be cooked we ate standing up right from the fridge, handfuls of Cool Whip, a whole jar of strawberry preserves, the bottle of Hershey's chocolate syrup. Whenever Lore left the house we headed straight for the fridge. It was like sneaking from Helene but not the same. It was more like wolfing than sneaking. Lore didn't like it, she shook her head and scolded and gave us the eyes rolled to the ceiling, but she kept buying us food and even took us to McDonald's once. I was fascinated with McDonald's, the squishy little burgers, the shakes, the Cokes so big you couldn't drink them all up.

The way to eat ice cream, the kind without stuff in it like chocolate chunks, is to microwave it first so it's soupy at the edges but not runny. Remember not to leave the spoon in the dish when you put it in the microwave.

There's not one grain of brown rice in Lore and Dean's house and neither one of them has ever had tofu or millet or seaweed or aduki beans or rice cakes or even yinnies. I can't say I miss any of that. I don't even know where to find a health food store in Las Vegas. I've never seen one. Lore goes to Safeway once a week with a long list, and we run and skip beside the shopping cart with her. She cooks every night and I don't have to help if I don't want to, but if I want to I can. Lore is from Germany and she taught me how to make sauerbraten but I didn't like it that much, the same with steak tartare. She makes us pork chops cooked in apple sauce, and ham glazed with pineapple, and stew with dumplings, and pot roast with little baby carrots cooked right alongside it.

School hot lunch isn't as exciting to me now that I can eat almost anything I want at home. We get a letter every month that has the school lunch menu printed on it for every school day. Monday is corn dogs, tater tots, and green salad. Tuesday is meat loaf, green beans, and whipped potatoes. Wednesday is pepperoni pizza and corn. Thursday is hamburgers, french fries, and carrot salad. Friday is chicken fingers, peas and carrots, and tater tots. You can have chocolate milk or regular. For dessert there's chocolate pudding or brownies or raisin cookies.

Chapter 29

Okay Ass, No Tits

I scuff my tennies on my way to English class, dreading it now when before I used to be okay with it. It was way too easy and not very interesting, but I brought books from home and put them in the pages of the class textbook to read while the class stuttered and stalled through stories by Jack London or O. Henry. I had been reading *All Quiet on the Western Front* and was loving it, and I never got behind in class. But I got too smart for my own good. Mrs. Tedesco had said, Some of you are having problems with language usage. Let's review some basic terms. Put your name and the date in the upper right hand corner of your paper. Write sentences using the terms on the board. I wrote a sentence using the word *becoming*. I wrote, You should wear beige more often, it's very becoming. Mrs. Tedesco called me up to her desk and said, This sentence is wrong. I said, Wrong how? She said, You failed to use *becoming* as a verb. I said, You didn't ask us to use *becoming* as a verb, you just said write a sentence using it. So I did. It's not wrong. She had looked frustrated and perplexed for a minute, considering. I knew that she knew that I knew I had used *becoming* wrong on purpose. To punish me, I guess, she put me in another class, the class I'm on my way to now this morning.

Mrs. Tedesco fried my goose good. She put me in an eighth grade class, and not just eighth grade but eighth grade gifted. I don't feel gifted, I feel cursed. The reading assignments are still easy, *To Kill a Mockingbird, The Last of the Mohicans, The Ballad of the Sad Cafe*. Raymond Carver and William Faulkner. The writing assignments aren't hard, book reports. It's the other kids in class that make this class hateful. We have to discuss our reading and writing in class, and the way I talk makes everyone think I'm a showoff. But it isn't my fault. The way I talk comes from books and that's the only way I know how to express myself. You have a contextualized understanding of that particular cultural milieu you have derived from literature, Lore said, rather than an experiential understanding of the culture of your peer group. Yeah, that's about it. And I don't know how to put on lip gloss either, because I was raised by wolves.

So my new English class. Even the room is bigger. I drudge my way up the steps and heave the door open and slide into my seat, plopping my backpack on the floor. I take out *To Kill a Mockingbird* and hunch into my seat and watch the rest of the class come in. The boys mostly wear glasses and act serious and don't spend hardly any time punching or kicking each other. The girls whisper quietly and pass notes, but they never do their hair or put on makeup. The desks are arranged four in a square facing each other to facilitate our discussion groups. The three other kids in my group totally and completely ignore me.

The teacher, Gary, not Mr. Gary, comes in and leans casually on his desk and says, Okay people, let's discuss the book reports. Anyone want to lead the discussion? Amy? Go ahead. Amy says, I liked the book because Scout is brave and smart. Yes, Amy, she is. Someone else says, I liked the part where the white man who lives with a black woman offers the whiskey to the kids but it turns out to be Coke. Yeah, that's right, this book is all about the prejudicial assumptions we make about one another. Someone asks, What is a chiffarobe exactly? and the class laughs. Um yes, go ahead, um, Claire. I say, The book has a peculiar tension. A peculiar tension in what way, Claire? Well, Scout is only six or so at the beginning of the book but she talks like her father the lawyer. The author is exercising her artistic license by having the protagonist speak in her father's tone. Gary looks at me. Very true, Claire, very observant. By now the rest of the class is shuffling their feet and squirming in their seats and looking bored. Okay everyone, pass your reports up to the front of the class. The girl across from me has written a note, What a showoff, with an arrow pointing at me, and she shows it to another boy and they smile. My face burns all the way through the rest of the class and on into lunch even.

At lunch I take my plastic tray and load it with a milk and silverware and a plate and I slide it along the metal rails in front of the steam table. A tired black lady in a hairnet spoons gravy onto my mashed potatoes. Creamy whipped potatoes, the menu always says. Then meat loaf and mixed vegetables and a brownie.

The walk across the cafeteria floor is a mile and I try to look nowhere while I pretend not to scan for a seat. Don't sit next to big groups. Don't sit next to groups of just guys or just girls. Don't sit next to eighth-graders. Don't sit next to Danny but sit where I can see him if I want to. That's another one in my list of how big public schools are different from small hippie ones, how the cafeteria and gyms are always so huge and how they seem to echo with tension. Slide into a space careful not to look right at anyone. Especially don't look at the group of girls wearing the see-through shirts and big slashes of blue and white eye shadow. What are you looking at, fish lips. Lookit the one with the banana nose. Okay ass but no tits, one says.

After eating I dump my tray and go outside onto the asphalt plain and watch people play tetherball. There's a forest of tetherball poles and a line of people waiting to play at each pole. I can hear the balls slap against the players' hands and whump against the pole after a big win, and a *thok* when someone serves. I'm wearing a red-flowered skirt and pink socks with tennis shoes and a blue wind breaker. No wonder no one wants to be friends with me. The tetherballs slap and thump and the kids yell and the bell rings loud but distant across the yard.

Chapter 30

Green Bean Casserole

For Thanksgiving we go to Uncle Chris's house here in Las Vegas. He moved from Ojo Sarco back to Las Vegas after the summer was over. He lives with his lady friend Ruthie and Ruthie's son who's four or five. They live in an apartment house on the cruddy side of town, all wineglass fences and drooping cottonwoods and bare yards full of old cars. Lore owns the apartments and rents them out. Dean is working so he stays home, Lore drives me and Haud over. She parks and we clamber out and Haud starts to chase the dog and I wander up the steps behind Lore. Ruthie greets us and hands Lore a vodka gimlet, and Chris hugs Lore, holding a can of beer. We're watching the fight, Chris says, giving me a hello squeeze. Come on in. Turkey should be ready soon.

I sit at the kitchen table and drink a generic brand of Coke out of a plastic cup and watch some of the fight from the corner of my eye. Huge sweating black men grunt and drive at each other and then collapse into their corners while the camera roves over thin blonde women wearing glitzy jewelry and fur coats on the sidelines. I can't watch the fight anymore. The men look so tired and so beaten I feel sorry for them. I watch the cottonwood tree outside. Groups of little kids kick a ball around in the dirt, cars cruise by slowly, playing loud music from their radios, the drivers calling to girls sitting on other porches. Lore's car looks tired, sitting in the dirt yard, Lore looks tired, Ruthie looks tired, wiping a strand of hair out of her eyes while bending over to look in the oven. Even the turkey looks tired, its drumsticks trussed together with cotton string, crumpled foil covering the top. There's green bean casserole to go with it, and cranberry sauce from a can, cut in slices. There's black olives, which Haud and I stick onto our fingers until Lore glares at us and then asks Ruthie for another gimlet.

Chapter 31

Try Chun King for a Beautiful Life

Some school mornings after leaving the house I go around the corner of our cul-de-sac and knock on the door of Vickie's house and we walk to the bus stop together. The wide street is quiet and empty of cars, everyone parks in their garages. A few drops of dew spot the hedges, drops of moisture run down the spires of the tall yucca plants, drops sparkle from a hairy head of cactus. The gravel that lines the drives crunches. Vickie's house is a lot like Lore's but has a two-story A-frame entrance, all dramatic, slanting panels of smoked glass and gray shale and heavy beams. In her yard there's yucca and red gravel, while Lore has evergreens and white gravel.

I ring the doorbell and it echoes in the entry and I hear the impatient *trip trip trip trip* of heels coming to the door. Vickie's mother answers, tanned skin and thinness and a shoulder-length feathered pageboy. She wears a white satiny robe with ruffles and white slippers with pouffy feathers at the toes and she looks down at me annoyed. Yes? Is Vickie here? I ask. She turns to call over her shoulder with her hand resting limply on the door, Vi-CKIE. Her robe flutters open and I see long smooth legs and the hairs over her veejay shaved in a tiny triangle.

Vickie comes to the door stuffing the last of a Pop-Tart into her mouth. Vickie is a smaller copy of her mom. Bouncy hair and tan with little white shoes clicking on the floor. She wears tight jeans with strawberries on the back pockets and a white tank top with strawberries on it and a white comb in her back pocket to match her top. She's so pretty and graceful and she chatters easily about nothing as we leave. What she had for breakfast, which was a Tab and six M&M's and half a Pop-Tart, how the green M&M's make you horny, how she gives herself fifteen minutes to shower and fifteen minutes to do her hair and fifteen minutes to do her makeup and fifteen minutes to dress and so it only takes her an hour to get ready in the morning. She says, For Christmas I want roller skates, the white booted kind, and a shorts outfit to skate in, white terry cloth with silver sparkle trim. Her mom won't buy her one, but she gets five dollars a week allowance and she's saving up for it herself. Your mom seemed mad, I say, and Vickie shrugs and says, She's always grumpy in the morning, she's a cocktail waitress and she doesn't like to get up early. Where does she work? Vickie gestures vaguely and says, The strip. Vickie and her mom are amazing to me. They make it look so easy, being a girl, being pretty girls. Me, I gave up. In the mornings I pull on whatever doesn't look too wrinkly, and even if I do take the time to agonize over my clothes there isn't much to choose from. I try to make my hair look like I didn't go to sleep with it wet, which is usually exactly what I did do. I want nice hair but I'd rather watch cartoons.

The bus comes, we slide into seats, Vickie chatters the whole way about anything, she's just kind of a nice hum in my ears, and I nod and smile. The bus bumps over train tracks and past warehouses toward our school, and the tin-colored sky meets the gray-brown desert along a horizon I can't quite see.

Chapter 32

Radio

The sound that you're hearing is only the sound of the low spark of high-heeled boys, heeled boys. A lopey song coming from my radio. For Christmas, Haud and I got matching transistor radios from Uncle Chris, perfect presents because they're great and they match so we can't argue about whose is better or bigger or cooler. New and shiny with plastic knobs and an antenna, fitting right in my hand, I can take it anywhere with me.

During Christmas break, which is called winter break, I spend a lot of time on the front steps listening to my radio under the unchanging sky. Blowing through the jasmine in my mind, this is for all the lonely people, sky rockets in flight, living it up at the Hotel California.

I sit with my legs tucked up under me and my chin resting on top of my knees. Ahead of me the even swoop of lawn, cut springy and short, going a little brown at the edges and center. The wide street is empty and quiet, the houses have their drapes pulled. I never see kids on our street except for a new family that moved in down the block. There's matching twins, a boy and a girl with blond hair. We play on their swing sometimes, and they have a gerbil. I had gone by Vickie's a few times but maybe she's visiting her dad.

Beside me on the steps are also my new roller skates, not the white booted kind I wanted that Vickie also wanted but the kind that clamp over your shoes. I've been scooting around the neighborhood, and Lady comes with me and I think she has a good time. I swear she almost barked once. If anyone in one of the low houses or long cars had seen me they would have seen a normal person, a kid with skates and a dog, a kid with clothes that matched and a dog and skates who lived in a normal house with normal parents who have jobs and wear shoes. I'm having a normal life, I think to myself with some surprise. I sleep in a bed with matching sheets, I take a shower every day, I eat normal food.

For days I roll through the neighborhood, the sound of my skates bouncing off closed garage doors. This neighborhood that doesn't seem to have any people in it, this city that doesn't have any weather or any smell, unless it's the smell of evergreens and cement and car exhaust. I push myself along onto larger streets where the traffic goes by in fast flashes and the sidewalk is wide and clean and crackless and treeless. No one in the cars sees me, and I stop, holding onto a streetlight so I don't roll, and wait for a light to change. I am completely anonymous. A long stream of cars goes by without change, the drivers only looking straight ahead. When the light changes I cross carefully and make it only to the median strip before the light changes again, and I'm stuck there like a target, the only thing made of flesh and blood in a sea of metal and glass and rubber and cement. I roll along until I'm at the mall, a bland strip of low buildings holding Mervyn's and Safeway and Vip's Big Boy and Sizzler Steakhouse and Michelin Tire center and the Garden Center and Kmart. I take off my skates and carry them through Mervyn's, looking at jewelry and clothes and stuffed animals and bathing suits and kitchenware and lawn furniture. With my allowance money I buy a gold chain, fake, with my initial on it, and a bottle of bubbles to blow on the lawn, and a pencil with a fuzzy troll on top. I eat an ice cream sitting on the curb, my skates next to me, all of a sudden having the funny idea that Helene is going to come right up to me and catch me eating shitfood.

Back at Lore's I take off my skates and go into the house for my radio and take it back on the steps. Fly like an eagle, the radio sings, let my spirit carry me. Then silence after I turn the radio off and listen to the very distant sound of traffic.

Christmas was fun. Mounds of crumpled wrapping paper littered the floor when we were done with our presents. Haud tore into his but I took my time. Ruthie gave me a little plastic purse with a nail file and nail polish. Lore gave me pants and two blouses that matched, blue corduroy pants and a see-through blouse of light blue and a dark blue turtleneck to go under the see-through one. The pants didn't fit, they were way too small, but I was embarrassed to tell Lore that. I still have the receipt, she said doubtfully, as I held my breath to close them. They're fine, I said, they're great. They were the same size as my old green bell-bottoms but they were way too small so I guess there's proof that I'm growing. Lore measured me and said, You're four feet and nine inches.

Haud and I bought presents for Lore, too. We got her a box of chocolates with cherry centers and a gold-plated necklace that came in a little white box with a cotton lining, all with money saved from our allowances. It was a real Christmas, which we never had before. Not quite a real tree because Dean waited until the last minute so there weren't any. We decorated Samantha, the rubber tree, and I thought she looked great. There was brunch afterwards with Chris and Ruth and my aunt Eve, who also gave me nail polishes and a little diary that closes with a lock and key. I'm having a normal life. We're going to have a party for New Year's Eve.

Without school I have plenty of time to read and I make trip after trip to Lore's big bookcase and forage for interesting titles. Kurt Vonnegut, *Slaughterhouse Five*, which I don't finish, and *One Flew Over the Cuckoo's Nest*, and Hunter S. Thompson about the Hell's Angels. Also *Joy of Sex*, which I look at for a long time and which I think looks gross but I keep on looking. The one I finish and then read again is called *The Diary of Mistress Anne* and it's about sexual bondage. This lady in spike heels and a black mask and a whip steps on men's penises and ties them up and stuffs things in their butts. She spanks them and makes them lick her shoes, gives them shock treatments and enemas.

Lore catches me with this one and says, I don't think you need to be reading this one just yet, and puts it up at the top shelf but she's not mean about it. It might be time for us to Have a Talk, she says, putting capitals on the words. What talk, I ask? She says, Clane, why don't you come into my room for a minute. We sit down at her vanity table and she says, I'm sure your mother never got around to telling you any of this but it's important. She brings out a notebook and pen and starts drawing me a picture. She says, Of course you're aware that men and women are different. Women have vaginas and uteruses as their reproductive apparatus and men have penises. I know all that, I say, beginning to squirm. Well, at some point in the future you're going to start getting your period. She draws me a picture of a uterus and fallopian tubes and cervix. She explains what's going to happen. Your uterus will fill up with blood that's a cushion and food for a baby. If you don't get pregnant, which God forbid you were to get pregnant at this age, the blood will come out of you once a month. I'm embarrassed and grossed out but I also feel important. I've never been in Lore's bedroom before.

I also look through Dean's record collection, lying on the floor in the living room in front of the lime-green sofa. Dean convinced Lore to make the living room more of a party room. There's a lava lamp and a black-light picture and a black light and sometimes they get stoned in there. I listen to Ravel's Bolero and to Edvard Grieg which is the Bugs Bunny music. I listen to the Rolling Stones and Devo. Lore thinks Dean's music and his posters are tacky but Dean says, mixing himself a martini, I'm a party animal. Do you kids want to know how to mix a Manhattan?

In the backyard I lift myself over the cinderblock wall that separates our yard from the vacant lot beyond. The torn earth stretches off into the distance to meet the long line of the shopping mall where I skate to and where we got Lore's presents. The dirt is softened into low hills where boys ride their dirt bikes over it. Clumps of mortar and cinderblock and iron bars lie in meaningless tangles. Twilight settles over the lot while I watch, planes fly overhead, low to the ground and winking their red and white lights.

On New Year's Eve Lore shows me how we're going to make champagne punch for the party. Take the big punch bowl down from the cupboard and carry it carefully to the bar and dust it. Unwrap a whole carton of lime sherbet, Haud says *sherbert*, and put it in the center of the bowl. I get sherbet on my hands and remember to wash my hands instead of wiping it on my pants. The champagne has been chilling all afternoon and Dean uncorks it and Haud and I watch while it fizzes all over. Pour the champagne over the top of the sherbet. It makes a frothy lime-green lake with a sherbet island in the center. In the kitchen Lore is making appetizers. She cooks chicken livers and wraps bacon around them and puts them on little silver skewers. She mixes dip and arranges crackers and cheese on a plate with little knives.

The doorbell rings. Guests. Clane, go answer the door and greet our guests and please conduct yourself like a young adult. There are Dean's coworkers from his office and Lore's coworkers from her school. There are friends from their church, which is Unitarian. Dean and Lore took us to their church and said, It's up to you whether you want to go to church or not. I didn't, not especially. There was miles of orange shag carpeting and a lot of old people. Unitarians sort of believe in everything. After the first time, I didn't go again and Lore doesn't go that often either.

Everyone at the party is old and I wander around listening to bits of conversation and saying, Hello, how do you do, when Lore says, This is my granddaughter Clane. Nice to meet you, Elaine, a stout lady with tightly curled gray hair and glasses tells me, bending down to shake my hand. Dean makes drinks at the bar, which is a real bar. Haud and I know how to make Dean and Lore's drinks, the shelves under the bar are lined with bourbon and gin and vodka and cordials and sherries and brandy. Strangely disturbing ubiquity, a woman is saying to Dean while he's handing her a drink. Dean nods and she sips her drink and goes on, I mean they were everywhere, and she gestures widely with her free hand. She's younger than the rest and dressed all in black. I stand at the bar near her, watching her painted fingernails clutch the stem of her martini glass, my chin on my hands, my perspective bobbing up and down as I chew cocktail nuts without taking my chin off my hands. Vast reaches of something

something, she says, her voice fading as I skip into the kitchen to check the clock.

The fluorescent lights under the cupboards are on, casting weird shadows on Lore's face as she puts more chicken liver things on a platter. She's moving carefully and says with a smile, I guess I'm a little tight. Lore is almost merry when she drinks, she throws her head back to laugh. She does this, tosses out a laugh, when the woman standing next to her says, Well it looked like a horse's ass to me but that's what I think about most modern art. I think your taste is utterly provincial, Lore says, But I couldn't agree more. I steal a handful of Maraschino cherries and listen to Chris and Matt talk about their motorcycles, with Haud hanging on every word. I'd rather have a sister in a whorehouse than a brother on a Honda, Haud says to them gleefully, and they look at me and say, Where did you kids learn to talk like that? Hunter S. Thompson, I say proudly, and run off to look at the champagne and sherbet lake.

Haud and I sneak some, though Lore would probably let us have some if we asked, and Dean definitely would. We go behind Samantha to drink it and listen to the grownups talking louder as they get drunker. Unexplained voices on the tape, someone says, An ominous gray-green color like the lizard twins, someone else says. Here, try some of this. It's only homegrown but it's better than that Colombian shit. Haud says to me from behind a sherbet mustache, I'm going to steal a roach from the ashtray and smoke it in the backyard. I stay behind the tree listening. I finished that first one when I came out of recovery, the woman in all black is saying. I found Clane reading it, Lore says. I peek from behind the tree and the lady in all black is the same lady who was on the cover of the Mistress Anne book. Mistress Anne is here in our house. Lore is holding a drink in one hand and a cigarette in the other and so is Mistress Anne and they are both wobbling a little bit. I think she's reading the *Joy of Sex* too, she's such a precocious child. I was too, Mistress Anne says, dragging deeply on her cigarette. Detox was a fucking nightmare, she goes on. All I could think about was floating aimlessly, like streams of radio waves. Waves crashing on the endless coastline of time. Would you care for another gin and tonic? Lore asks. The room is full of people talking and some of them are bobbing and gyrating because Dean has put Dance Machine on the record player.

I steal a tiny bit more punch and no one notices even though I spill some on the dog. Lady is under the bar eating cocktail nuts spilled on the floor, maybe Haud left the back door open went he went to steal his roach. Lady licks some punch from the floor and this makes me laugh, to think of Lady getting drunk, maybe she would have more personality as a drunk dog. Haud suddenly sticks his head up from behind the bar where he's been crouching, trying out different liquors. Chartreuse is one hundred and eighty proof, he says, holding the bottle, looking at it with first one eye closed and then the other. His eyes are shiny and glazed. I think I'm gonna puke he says, and weaves blindly to the sliding glass doors. Lady follows him and gets tangled up in his legs. He throws up all over her and she looks up at him, polite and confused, with foamy green champagne barf sliding down the side of her head. She wags her tail uncertainly and Haud staggers to a lawn chair and flops onto it face-first and doesn't move.

Back in the living room I find the big recliner in the corner and it's empty and I sink back into it and listen to the drifts and eddies of noise, people talking, the music, the television on.

The hypocrisy of disco, you know, because it's all totally ripped off from soul music but cleaned up so it won't scare whitey. How are you so political about music, man? All you ever listen to is Led Zeppelin. That's not true, I had all those Herbie Hancock reel-to-reels. What do you think about eight- track? Well it depends on the speakers. No it depends on your amp, man, its all about the amps. These are Bang and Olufsen. And here's the Strip from the Las Vegas sky pilot, boy look at all those lights, folks, what a beautiful sight for us in this new decade. All this talk about cultural disintegration in the shadow of the bomb is laziness, it's sheer intellectual laziness because if you read your history life was much more difficult in the Middle Ages. Wars, diseases, plague, starvation, invading armies. She told me that macrame helped to settle her nerves. Did you read *The Serial?* Hysterically funny, not as funny as…Try Chun King for a beautiful body try Chun King for a beautiful life. Dean thinks he's turned this room into a party pit, but wouldn't you agree it's just... Do ya think I'm sexy, come on baby let me know.

Chapter 33

The Sky Is Very Far Away

I found Haud passed out on a lawn chair this morning,
Lore says the next day over a late brunch. Brunch is halfway
between breakfast and lunch. I like that word, brunch. It has bite
to it. Ha-ha, I think to myself, a word about food that has bite. I
reach for more orange juice. We're all tired from last night's party.
Dean and Lore have lines deeply etched around their eyes. I feel
sorry for Haud. He's still sleeping, now in our room. The house
seems large and quiet and subdued. The floor this morning was a
sticky plain of cigarette butts, empty and partly full glasses, and
crumpled napkins. The punch glasses had a curdled film in them,
and some of the napkins held smears of lipstick or half-eaten
chicken livers congealed in bacon fat. Hee hee, I laugh to myself,
Haud barfed on the dog. I didn't tell Lore about it. I told Matt,
though.

Matt was sleeping on the sofa in the sewing room, which
is also Lore's office and is near our room. He was as passed-out as
Haud and he had a black eye and a big lump on his forehead.
What happened to you? I asked, sitting on the arm of the sofa
and poking him lightly with my toe in the shoulder. He had slept
in his clothes and the room had a sour smell and his eyes were
puffy and one was swelled shut. I heard you talking in here with

Lore last night. Matt sat up groggy and touched his forehead and groaned. He swung his legs off the sofa and stood up and then sat back down and put his head in his hands. I wrecked my car last night and Lore had to bail me out of jail. That's what you heard us talking about. I don't know which is worse, my hangover or Lore's wrath. He turned and grinned at me and I was glad to see there was still some life in him and I went to go see about cartoons but there wasn't any. When Lore came into the kitchen I was eating cereal and watching *Solid Gold*. Save some appetite for brunch, she said, not too grumpily. Matt's waking up, I said. She harumphed and I knew not to ask more. I thought it was Claude, I thought Claude was here, I said. No, your father is not only not here, he hasn't called, either. Your father, from what I understand, is in Albuquerque, but he has not found the time to call and inquire after his children.

After brunch I help with the dishes and I help clean up from the party, putting away records and emptying ashtrays. I take my roller skates outside and spend the rest of the day zooming around the neighborhood through the smell of car exhaust and cement and evergreen. Scraping up and down the wide sidewalks, the only sound I hear is my own breathing. The sky is a million miles above me and the streets narrow ahead of me to tiny dark points and then vanish. Today is the first day of 1980.

Chapter 34

The Year of Becoming Thirteen

Those are some tight pants alright, someone snickers, an older boy on the bus. I pretend not to hear but my face is hot. The pants Lore got me for Christmas. The bus bounces past a convenience store, past a vacant lot full of trash. On the news it said, Authorities have been discovering dismembered human remains in trash bags in vacant lots throughout the city. What is the meaning of this grisly phenomenon? the news man asked with a serious expression. The bus grinds through intersections and stops at train tracks.

Being back at school after break is just plain weird. I'm used to school now, used to the math classes I'm failing, used to the English classes I hate, used to the steaming cafeteria food and the meanness of the cafeteria itself. I'm used to not having any friends. At first I thought that since I live in a normal house and wear normal clothes and eat normal food and have an allowance like everyone else that I would get along with everyone else. My outside looks like everyone else's outside, and I thought that meant it would be Okay. But for reasons I don't know, I don't fit in with everyone else.

So I ride the bus and I go to my classes and I hang from the chain-link fence on the yard. I watch girls share combs and lip glosses and pass notes and brush their hair. I watch for Danny with his silky brown hair and sweet eyes like a doe and never talk to him. I struggle along with geometry, arcs and tangents and planes, hating it silently, and I write papers that say, Answer in your own words, what would you most like to be when you grow up? I don't have any idea at all what I want to be when I grow up. I eat hamburgers and creamy whipped potatoes and drink chocolate milk.

In the school yearbook there is a picture me and others running on the yard, playing flag football, and I am the dark ugly one, with eyes too big and nose and mouth too big and too much hair flying around my face. My jacket is falling off my shoulders and my socks are slipping down.

Violence at school. It starts with a talent show, which is performed by the eighth-graders and watched by the rest of us in the cafeteria and on closed-circuit TV in the other classrooms. Girls twirl batons and do cheerleading routines. Someone plays violin, someone else plays piano. A boy with stringy hair plays air guitar to Lynyrd Skynyrd. A skinny boy in glasses does magic tricks. Twelve black girls do a dance to a disco song, each of them wearing a shirt that has their sign of the zodiac on the front in glittery swirls. When the winner is announced and it's the magician, who did his tricks right in front of the judges' stand, the black girls start screaming and cursing and one of them pulls the plug on the video camera. A counselor shoulders one of the black girls out of the way and three more of the girls fall on him, screeching and kicking and pulling his hair. His glasses falling off, his jacket flapping open, the counselor falls over a table and the girls jeer at him. Judges are running for the doors and kids are jumping out of their seats, fists pumping, eyes wild. The disco girls turn their stereo on again loud in the confusion and everyone starts dancing while two girls smack around the magician boy, who is cowering under his coat and pleading, I'm sorry I'm sorry I'm sorry hey hey don't don't.

Fights at lunch. Big mean-looking white girls with slashes of blue eye shadow and dark plum blush angled across their cheeks flail at each other's hair and shirts and faces. You slut you bitch you whore, they scream at each other while a crowd of kids gathers around them yelling, Fight fight fight. The girls don't punch, they slap and swarm and push. One girl has a fistful of the other's hair and one has a clutch of the other's blouse, which rips and the girl screeches desperately, trying to cover her chest while swinging wildly at the other girl's head. They roll around on the ground and one comes up with a bleeding face. No teachers come to pull them apart and after a few minutes of frenzied thrashing it's just over and the girls break off into opposite directions, one girl rushing into the bathroom with a crowd of girls following saying, You kicked her ass you kicked her ASS. In the bathroom the fluorescent light stutters on the crowd of girls. The girl who's been fighting has small hard boobs jutting from her too-tight shirt and she brushes her hair and shakes it back nervously and shakily, flushed from the energy of the fight.

Violence at home. Lore has received my report card in the mail about failing math, and there will be no TV, no roller-skating, no music, and no reading until I relearn my times tables and learn by heart the basic math terms from the back of the book, like *polynomial* and *ratio* and *divisor*. We sit at the dining room table going, What's six times eight? What's six times nine? and she glints at me, her gaze as sharp as broken glass, this is the violence of it, her gaze. I'm crying and it's not because I don't know my times tables, it's because of Lore. She has begun to fill me with dread just by the way she walks into a room. Great hitching sobs fill my chest and she looks at me like I'm a bug. She puts the flash cards down on the table and looks at the ceiling and goes, Oh really, Clane.

I can't do it, I don't know how, I gasp, gulping for air. I never had any math. It's not fair, I never had to go to school before. Helene didn't make me. Just pull yourself together, she says, your self-pity is disgusting. It's not self-pity, I say, it's not. It's not fair, none of you are fair, Helene and… Lore cuts me off, saying, We're not talking about your mother here. We're talking about your attention to arithmetic. We're not talking about your mother or your father or your pooooor deprived life. Whooooo ever told you life was going to be fair? It's tough all over, get used to it. I know you can be very capable when you want to be.

There's not an ounce of warmth in that glance like broken glass and the voice that mocks this terrible pain welling up in me. She's talking about math but I'm not. My dread, my aching lostness and humiliation, have nothing to do with math. What it is instead is this whole past year, the year of becoming thirteen, the process of it. I am beginning to know something I didn't know before, a terrible thing. The awful thing that I'm learning is that even though where I am changes all the time, who I'm with changes all the time, everything happening outside of me will be forever changing, but one thing inside of me never changes, my constant longing for something I don't have or someone who's not there or someplace I am not. Bare feet in a dusty road lined with blackberry bushes, a sun-warmed dirty-kid smell, purple clouds gathering over a valley. Poplars swaying, grape Nehi, Claude driving forever down the road with silvery holes for eyes. Ki somewhere, Helene somewhere, Claude somewhere, Random somewhere. Lore's right, I know, life isn't fair, but the way she says it mocks the simple pain of knowing that simple thing.

Lore sends me into my room to calm down and calls Haud to start with flash cards. My eyes ache, I'm exhausted with crying. I listen to them in the dining room. What's five times seven? Ahdahno. What's five times four? Ahdahno. What's four times two? Ahdahno. Oh for CHRISTS sake stop that fidgeting. If she hates us so much why did she let us come live with her?

Chapter 35

Disintegration

Across the room Haud says, Clane what are you doing under the covers with the flashlight? and I say, READING so shut up.

I picked a pamphlet up off the ground once, it said "Your Body and You." It had pictures and it explained how boys and girls masturbate. For boys it was practically a how-to manual but for girls it just said they masturbate by rubbing their thighs together. That's the dumbest thing I ever heard. It's best if you use the detachable shower head. Make sure you lock the bathroom door first.

I had been writing about this in the little diary with a lock on it that I got for Christmas and Haud read it and I know he did because there was a smear of chocolate on one of the pages. Haud has been obsessed with making M&M's melt in his hand lately so he could sue the company for false advertising.

So here is my diary with its ugly scrawled writing and Haud's pawprint on it and I bet he let his scummy friend Derek read it too. First on my list of things to do this morning is kill Haud. I go to trap him in his covers and pummel him but he wriggles away and makes a run for the backyard, where he tries to hide behind first the fig tree and then the marijuana plant that Dean and Lore let him grow but which is now dying, nearly dead, covered in yellow leaves, because he over fertilized it. Fucking whoredog! I scream at Haud, yanking at the back of his shirt. When he turns to run in the other direction, I punch him hard in the stomach and then he's crying, Lore, Clane hit me for no reason. Lore is standing in the open door with one hand holding her cigarette up in the air and the other on her hip. I say accusingly, He read my diary. That is no reason to hit your brother. I stomp off and Haud keeps crying, crumpled up in the dirt next to his dead plant, holding his stomach, which the next day has big bruises on it.

After this I start to notice that Haud has gone from being just a weird kid to being a bad kid. Was it because I always hit him? He used to steal roaches from Lore or Dean's ashtrays to smoke, but now he steals from their stash for real. He's always stoned. He's not even eleven and he's always high. He's droopy stoned all of the time or overdosed on B vitamins because he heard they give you energy, so he takes handfuls of them and can't sleep at night and then sleeps all day in class or barfs up B vitamins all over his desk at school. Lore can't figure out what's wrong with him and takes him to the doctor. Hark who goes there, stop or I'll shoot, stop or I'll shoot, he yells, running around with a plastic sword he bought at the mall.

Maybe he's disturbed, Lore is saying to her friend Mabel or Mavis or Gladys on the phone, the lady from the party with steel-gray hair who called me Elaine. Maybe he's disturbed and I should take him to a psychologist. Silence while she listens to the phone. He was essentially abandoned by his mother, who never liked him, she goes on, and practically abandoned by his father, who's totally irresponsible. The kid's a wreck, I think to myself, and it's my fault because I hit him. Helene didn't like him and Claude didn't take care of him and I should have but instead I hit him.

Haud doesn't go to school for days no matter what Lore threatens him with, and he keeps stealing her pot and he and his scummy friend let themselves into the house during the day when they're supposed to be at school to chug chartreuse and cordial from the bar. They steal loose change, they steal my collection of lunch money and allowance I've been saving for roller skates, the white booted kind. He and his friend with the ratty eyes go out into the vacant lot behind the house and huff the gas from whipped cream cans and then they huff paint cans and markers. They lie in the hollowed troughs between the melted dirt piles and drink cough syrup and cranberry cordial.

Lore freaks out and gives us both an inquisition when she notices the almost empty liquor bottles. I can't say anything about my stolen allowance and lunch money because I'm not supposed to save my lunch money, and my silence in the face of Haud's obvious fucked-upness makes me an accomplice. She thinks I'm stealing pot and liquor too, I'm not, all I've been doing is masturbating and reading the *Joy of Sex* and Marquis de Sade and Marquis de Sade isn't that good anyway, who would want to be deflowered with a candle?

Something is disintegrating here. I feel it in the way the room gets colder when Lore enters it, and I can feel it in the silence at the dinner table where Haud slumps red-eyed over his pork chops.

On the phone to uncle Matt, Lore says, Can you please spend some time with these children? This is just wearing me out. Granted, Haud is eight years younger than you were when I started having trouble with you but maybe he could use a male influence.

Matt comes over on a Saturday morning with Debbie and his truck full of inflated inner tubes and a thermos of hot chocolate. We drive out of the city up to some mountains, all sharing the front of the truck. Matt has a can of Bud between his legs and Debbie rolls a joint while he drives and they smoke it. As we drive higher there's rain and it spats against the windshield and the radio plays Electric Light Orchestra and the cab is filled with the rich sounds of a symphony. We climb higher into snow and park at the base of a hill. All day long we trudge the inner tubes up the hill and then fling ourselves onto them belly-first and slide and swing and whirl down the snow-covered hill, jouncing and yelling and spinning.

Other Saturdays Matt and Debbie show up and we drive to Redrock and climb around on the rocks all day. This is called bouldering, Matt says, taking off his shoes to climb. Follow me and do what I do. We haul ourselves up and around rocks, clinging like lizards to the sides of the boulders. I get scared but keep climbing and Haud does too and then we're back at the bottom, flushed and triumphant. Matt sits at the base of a rock drinking a Coors with one hand on Debbie's thigh while Debbie snorts white powder off the mirror of her makeup compact. She rubs her finger across the mirror and then across her teeth and gums and says, Cocaine makes your mouth numb, you can give blowjobs for hours. Don't tell your grandma I said that. Can I have some? Haud asks hopefully. No, they both say at once, these are grownup drugs and you shouldn't even be smoking pot. You want to grow up to be a loser like me? Matt says, growling. We drive back and Matt lets me steer while he drives, and the radio sings, Go on take the money and run.

Matt's male influence doesn't change anything. Whatever I leave lying around, like a fake turquoise ring Ruthie gave me, disappears and then Haud has five dollars and like magic Derek shows up, Derek with his greasy tangle of dirty blond hair. Want to go over to the mall and play pinball? they ask, and I say no, covering my book with my hands, which is a Stephen King book, *Carrie*, open to the part where the girl and the guy are doing it in the back of his truck. Haud curls his lip at me and Derek gives me a crooked knowing grin.

I'm scared sometimes that Haud will die and I wake up in the middle of the night and cross our room to his bed when I can't hear his breathing. I crouch near him and listen for his breath to make sure, my head near his mouth. I have never given up trying to make my survival something interesting, something that has funny parts and even beauty or magic but it must have been a long time ago that Haud did, gave up, stopped trying. Like it's not easy holding your pee all night because you don't want to go to the outhouse in the cold dark, but if you do, there's dew on the lilacs near the outhouse. But Haud would just pee in his bed instead of holding it and then sleep in the wet pee, and if Claude smelled the pee he would cuff Haud and make him hang the sleeping bag over a tree. This is maybe the difference between me and Haud.

It must have been when Haud was about four, he couldn't tie his own shoes yet and he would walk around all day saying, Somebody tie my *shoe*, somebody tie my *shoe*, like a tuneless song. Someone would get mad at him for being obnoxious and hit him and then he'd spend the rest of the day playing by himself. Me, I would learn how to tie my shoes and then someone would say, Look how great Clane is, she tied her own shoes, but Haud didn't figure out that you could do that, get loves and pets for doing something right instead of doing it wrong. And I learned how to lie and sneak well to get what I wanted but Haud has no guile and is a bad liar. Haud got cheated somehow so I crouch over his bed at night to make sure he is still breathing, as if it's another thing he can't do for himself or will fuck up.

Meanwhile Lore is getting angrier and angrier with Haud and more impatient with me and things are falling apart. I don't know what it is that's falling apart because I can't put my finger on what it was that used to be whole, but now that it is falling apart I can feel pieces of it whirling away into a hole. Dislocation.

Chapter 36

Weightless

In March it's my birthday and Lore has a party for me, I'm thirteen. I'm a teenager now. Not that this was something I was looking forward to, I didn't really think about it. I guess it only hits me at the party when someone says it, Hey Clane, you're a teenager now.

The party is me and Haud and Lore and Dean and Matt and Chris and Eve. It's a late afternoon dinner on Sunday and I get to sit at the head of the table where Dean usually sits. There is a cake with candles on it and when I blow them out they relight and keep relighting and everyone hollers along with me and this makes me feel good, merry laughter around the table. I'm having a normal life. Lore tells me to close my eyes and not open them until she says to. I'm delighted with the role I get to play, all me. When I open my eyes there's a brand-new bicycle resting on its kickstand right in front of me. A Schwinn, gleaming new. It's a cruiser and not a three-speed but I keep that disappointment hidden.

The biggest present Lore saves for last. It's a package from Helene. We're all still seated around the table eating cake and looking at my bike and there in front of me is a parcel wrapped in brown paper, an old grocery bag, tied in string, my mom's familiar spidery handwriting. There's a hollow windy excitement deep in my chest, the sense of something big and significant. Huge questions will be answered, meaning will be made, past and present will be mapped out on straight lines. I will open the package to reveal some deep truth about the past and a map for the future. This goes through my head in a series of emotional flashes as I look at the package.

I open it and first inside is a yellow tee shirt that has a picture of an elephant raging through a field of huge pot plants. The shirt says, Hawaiian Poccololo. Wrapped in the tee shirt is a joint, a fat one decorated in bright colors from a felt-tip pen, flowers and moons and mandalas. Let's smoke it, Haud says, and Light her up, Claaaaane, Matt says. Dean ceremoniously presents me with his gold Dunhill lighter and I light the joint and take a deep drag and pass it along the table and everyone has some.

Almost immediately the room, which is bright with the pretty yellowy afternoon light that slants through the drapes, feels thick with a glowing liquid that I can breathe, like the air has turned to ochre. Viscous golden air suspends the colors of the motes drifting through the sliding glass door and, like when you're in the bathtub, sounds seem louder but also like they come from a long way off. Time stops, people's mouths move, open and close, but the sounds they make take forever to reach me across the sea of golden light. It takes me ten or twenty minutes to turn my head just a slight fraction to the left and the movement of my head causes a cosmic sonic boom in the universe that explodes in slow-motion sound. When I can pick apart the sounds caused by the sonic boom, what I hear is the high tuneless whistling of wind blowing endlessly without pattern across fields of tall grass, the ceaseless song of an unending distance without meaning. I concentrate all of my attention on this sound, lonely and keening, the oddly familiar song of slowed time, serene emptiness, the feeling of forever and nowhere.

   After another hour real sounds seep back into my ears and my eyes come back into focus, but I can't make any sense of what anyone is saying. I watch people's mouths move and sounds come out but in some other language I can't understand right now. Filled with slow-moving immense panic, I try to do something normal, pick my hand up from the table and move it toward a fork, move the fork toward my plate, fumble a piece of cake onto the fork, another hour to get the cake to my mouth. My mouth is too dry to eat the cake and I move the dry heavy mess around in my mouth for another endless amount of time until I can swallow it, and then comes the unbelievable difficulty of moving my hand toward my glass of milk, getting the glass to my mouth. Swallow. Another hour to move my tongue around the inside of my mouth. I'm grinning like an idiot, I realize, but no one seems to notice.

I look away from the hidden meaning of people's faces into my own lap and feel vertigo as the planet tilts slowly on its axis, spinning slow and grand in space. As it revolves, my eyes on my hands in my lap, a whole day goes by, the planet moves from light through degrees of shade and then the other half is in darkness. Across the globe whole lives are being led while I move my hands to the table again, reach for my fork again. Cars wait in traffic on freeways and the drivers hang their arms out of open windows, people replace telephone receivers and look out windows, a dog chases a Frisbee in slow-motion across a field, myriad things acting in constant random continuity.

Someone turns a light on in the room as it starts to get dark outside and I catch my own reflection in the sliding glass door, and for just that one instant I perceive myself to be beautiful, my own face, just as it is, shining with its own interior light. Another door opens and Lore comes in, bringing her own chill. My mind stutters over images of Haud drowning in blood, my mother screaming when Ki was born, Ki crying in a dark jungle, horror and remorse, the overwhelming understanding that there is a veil over everything, the wrongness behind the veil. This is the truth, the veil of wrongness over everything.

Maybe hours pass, maybe minutes, but the pot leaves me in slow waves. I sink into the big chair in the living room, happy to think about nothing. I'm never smoking pot again. I read Helene's letter.

She is in Hawaii with Tom Starchild. There is no mention of Ki or why she went to Hawaii. She is contemplating the perfection of a field of kudzu at dusk when the cranes rise, in the shadow of a mountain called the sleeping goddess. No mention of when she will return or what she's doing there. No mystery is resolved, no questions are answered. I can barely read her writing, and what she says makes almost no sense to me. I can't imagine her life and I guess I don't care. I feel emptied out. That is what thirteen feels like to me, a year in which everything became very large and somehow quiet, as if sounds happened a long way off from me and weren't connected to me in any direct way. I try to think for a minute where I was this same time, my birthday, a year ago, and I can't be sure exactly, maybe the abandoned ranch, maybe Sugarloaf mountain. A year starting in hot silence and isolation and ending in this city of blank spaces growing randomly in the desert. A year filled with different places but mostly filled with the space between places. I understand now that I live in those spaces between places, not tethered by anyone or anything.

Later in the evening I sit on the front steps with my radio, listening to songs but also to the hiss and crackle of places on the radio with no station. Blowing through the jasmine in my mind. I was dreaming of the night, would it turn out right. I'm not thinking about much, not anything really. Lore has told us we're going back to live with our dad again, we can live in Albuquerque with him, we'll get settled down. I know we won't. I'm thirteen and weightless. I belong nowhere.

The End